Routledge American History Series

JOHN HOPE FRANKLIN & ABRAHAM S. EISENSTADT, *Editors*

Routledge American History Series
JOHN HOPE FRANKLIN & ABRAHAM S. EISENSTADT, *Editors*

Paul A. Carter
NORTHERN ILLINOIS UNIVERSITY

The Twenties
in America

London
ROUTLEDGE AND KEGAN PAUL LTD

First published in Great Britain 1968
by Routledge & Kegan Paul Limited
Broadway House, 68-74 Carter Lane
London, E.C.4

Printed in Great Britain by
Lowe & Brydone (Printers) Ltd., London

SBN 7100 6308 3   Cloth
          6309 1   Paper

Owing to production
delays this book was
published in 1969

For Christina, Brian, and Bruce,
born in the Sixties under LBJ,
and not at all impressed that
their father was born under
Calvin Coolidge

EDITORS' FOREWORD

It is a commonplace that each age writes its own history, for the reason that man sees the past in the foreshortened perspective of his own experience. This has certainly been true of the writing of American history. The purpose of our historical writing remains constant: to offer us a more certain sense of where we are going by indicating the road we have taken in getting there. But it is precisely because our own generation is redefining its direction, the way other generations have redefined theirs before us, that the substance of our historical writing is changing. We are thinking anew of our direction because of our newer values and premises, our newer sense of how we can best fulfill the goals of our society, our newer outlook on the meaning of American life. Thus, the vitality of the present inspires the vitality of our writing about the past.

It is the plan of the *Crowell American History Series* to offer the reader a survey of the point of arrival of recent scholarship on the central themes and problems of American history. The scholars we have invited to do the respective volumes of the series are younger individuals whose monographs have been well received by their peers and who have demonstrated their mastery of the subjects on which they are writing. The author of each volume has undertaken to present a summation of the principal lines of discussion that historians of a particular subject have been pursuing. However, he has not written a mere digest of historical literature. The author has been concerned to offer the reader a sufficient factual and narrative account to help him perceive the larger dimensions of the subject. Each author, moreover, has arrived at his own conclusions about those aspects of his subject

vii

that have been matters of difference and controversy. In effect, he has written not only about where the subject stands in historiography but also about where he himself stands on the subject. And each volume concludes with an extensive critical essay on authorities.

The books in this series are designed for use in the basic course in American history, although they could be used, with great benefit, in advanced courses as well. Such a series has a particular utility in times such as these, when the traditional format of our American history courses is being altered to accommodate a greater diversity of texts and reading materials. The series offers a number of distinct advantages. It extends and deepens the dimensions of course work in American history. In proceeding beyond the confines of the traditional textbook, it makes clear that the study of our past is, more than the student might otherwise infer, at once complex, sophisticated, and profound. It presents American history as a subject of continuing vitality and fresh investigation. The work of experts in their respective fields, it opens up to the student the rich findings of historical inquiry. It invites the student to join with his older and more experienced colleagues in pondering anew the major themes and problems of our past. It challenges the student to participate actively in exploring American history and to seek out its wider reaches on his own.

John Hope Franklin
Abraham S. Eisenstadt

CONTENTS

We utterly decline to be pioneers of a new age, or apostles of a new faith, or martyrs of a new war. We refuse to be psycho-analyzed. Most of us are just rather ignorant, fairly moral, quite intelligent young people, with a sense of humor and normal interests. We try to learn something from our elders but are hopelessly misled. We have open eyes, but no convictions. We don't believe politicians or preachers, but we behave as respectfully as possible and hide our smiles.

PHILIP GIBBS, *The Age of Reason* (1928)

ONE

Of Bohemians and Consumers

We stand at an awkward distance from the years we name the Twenties. We are not quite near enough to feel their relevance to our contemporary condition, in the way we feel the relevance of the New Deal or of the 1941 war in the Pacific; and yet we are not quite far enough away to view the decade from 1919 to 1929 with the same detachment that we contemplate the culture of the Gilded Age or the politics of Henry Clay.

No doubt this awkwardness will pass. The generation that experienced the Twenties has been giving place for some time now to one that has only been told about them. The turning point may have been reached in 1960, when Irving Bernstein wrote: "The present world is so far removed from the world of the twenties . . . that many who did not live through the earlier times . . . refuse to believe things were so different." Conceivably a still younger generation of students may be ready to relegate the Twenties from the realm of "experience," felt as real, to the never-never land of "history" as depicted in reproductions on schoolroom walls, with George Washington (in profile) eternally crossing the Delaware.

The historian in his vocation as teacher tries to convince his hearers, caught up in the concerns of the subjective present, that what they do not remember nevertheless actually happened —but historians are themselves caught up in the cycle of remembering and forgetting. So, the student who would understand the Twenties ought to consult accounts both old and new: for example, both Frederick Lewis Allen, writing in 1931 when the events of the previous decade had in truth taken place *Only Yesterday,* and John D. Hicks, recalling that age of *Republican Ascendancy* thirty years afterward. Such accounts support and correct each other, and newest is not necessarily truest.

In his preface to William E. Leuchtenburg's *The Perils of Prosperity 1914–32,* written in 1958, Daniel Boorstin credited the author with "the advantage of being too young to lose objectivity through his own recollections." But Leuchtenburg himself had high praise for the older work by Allen, "written," he said, "in such a lively style that academicians often underrate its soundness." True, we do need the balancing insights of the younger writer, who, in Boorstin's words, "reconstructs the . . . spirit of the age from its documents." But we need also the perspective of immediacy. Preston Slosson's *The Great Crusade and After,* for example, written in 1930 when the Prohibition amendment was a seemingly permanent part of the Constitution and when the automobile was still a comparative novelty, expresses a side of the Twenties which for readers since the onset of Repeal and smog control would otherwise be irrecoverable. And historiography has room and need also for emotion recollected, not necessarily in tranquillity, as in Hicks.

One complication arises at the very outset, both for students of history who remember the Twenties and for those who do not: the fact that last impressions, contrary to the popular belief, tend to be more vivid than first ones. A fair number of persons whose careers spanned the years from 1919 to 1929 were active, or at least visible and articulate, in the public life of the Fifties and even into the Sixties. The Hoovers, Herbert and J. Edgar; Upton Sinclair and Ezra Pound; Walter Lippmann and David Lawrence; Felix Frankfurter and John Dos Passos; Louis Armstrong and Maurice Chevalier; the Four Horsemen and Jack Dempsey—examples could be multiplied manyfold, and in every case our after-image of the older man hovers between us and the incarnation of his younger self. The child is father to the man, but in the man we forget the child.

Conversely, men of one generation who remain busy and even useful into a later day are sometimes disconcerted to find themselves treated as part of "history," a treatment which, as Henry F. May has observed, the subjects commonly do not find flattering: "One survivor of the period says that instead of being revived, it is being excavated like a ruin, and another complains that he and his friends are already being preserved in complete bibliographies while yet, as far as they can tell, alive." In his autobiography *More Lives Than One,* Joseph Wood Krutch declared that when an attractive girl student who was writing a paper on American literature came to his office in Columbia University and said she had "been told that . . . well, that *you* were *alive* during the F. Scott Fitzgerald period," he decided it was time to retire!

He might also have told the young lady that, once she had begun to deal with her subject in abstraction as "the Fitzgerald Period," the battle was already more than half lost. The present writer once sent a copy of an article on Senator Thomas J. Walsh of Montana, a prominent Democratic Party spokesman in the Twenties, to an aged and dear friend who had been well acquainted with the senator; with the candor of eighty years the recipient replied that she had enjoyed reading the journal, "and marveled again at the ability of trained historians to destroy almost completely the memory of persons known to the reader." Every young historian should occasionally be brought up short in this fashion; for the professional preparation of doctoral candidates for scholarly work in the history of periods prior to their own conscious lifetimes has been described by one reviewer as consisting of reading a great many old newspapers without ever quite understanding them.

Distance from a man, an event, or a movement *may* grant detachment; that is why "contemporary history" cannot really be written as History. But distance can also deceive, either by blocking the vision of the observer with images of the intervening terrain or by blurring the further landscape in heat-haze. Charles G. Sellers has written of "Andrew Jackson versus the historians" in words that apply with equal force to the Twenties: "The succession of frames of reference and the multiplication of hypotheses can distort as well as amplify the past."

If distance can distort, it can also enchant. In a *Harper's* article of 1954, "The Spirit of Our Times," Lovell Thompson sternly warned the older generation of his day against surrender to nostalgia about the Twenties: "In spite of its wisdom, age is always deceived by its infirmity into seeing a virtue in the folly of its youth because that youth was associated with health." But if enchantment can distort one's vision of the past, so can disenchantment; the same infirmity which deceives age into seeing virtue in the folly of its youth can also deceive it into seeing folly in its youthful aspirations. If F. Scott Fitzgerald remained "young to the bitter end," as one post-mortem essayist put it, a great many other people seem to have come out of the Twenties in the same frame of mind in which they might have come out of a speakeasy, vowing "Never again!"

This sad and sober repudiation of the Twenties has had

at least as much publicity as the nostalgia of which Lovell Thompson complained. Thus the most recent revision of Morison and Commager's textbook *Growth of the American Republic* left untouched its authors' earlier judgment on the Twenties: "Seldom has a generation bequeathed so little that was of permanent value and so much that was troublesome to the future." The chapter to which this statement was prefatory went on to chronicle a great deal which nevertheless might be considered of permanent value—the comic genius of Charles Chaplin, the poetry of Frost and Eliot and Sandburg, the theater of O'Neill, and last but surely not least the historical scholarship of Turner and Parrington and Allan Nevins. So even the grand simplicities of a textbook, it would seem, break down before the problem of the Twenties. Every generalization one makes about the period has a disconcerting way of turning into its opposite.

What confronts us here is not so much a batch of old newspapers as a kind of palimpsest, so often scrubbed and scribbled over that the *Ur*-text at the bottom is all but lost. The scribbles include slogans: "Jazz Age," "Normalcy," "Lost Generation." In his own memoir of the period, Matthew Josephson called one of the most famous among these slogans a "monumental misnomer," born of Gertrude Stein's momentary petulance at a few party-crashers: "We must dispose of the fallacy of the Lost Generation once and for all," Josephson concluded. And even though he conceded Lovell Thompson's essential point—"No doubt because of the onset of age most of us think of that time as a very diverting and carefree period and so 'happier' than the present"—the historian, old or young, must also reckon with the possibility that it really *was* a diverting and carefree period for some of these people. Certainly one finds in the reminiscences of men otherwise quite different in temperament and ideology considerable evidence that alongside the "lostness" there does seem to have been a good deal of joy.

Ernest Hemingway remembered the circumstances of Miss Stein's famous remark quite differently from Josephson's ac-

count, and his posthumously published *A Moveable Feast* ended
with the testimony: "This is how Paris was in the early days when
we were very poor and very happy." "It wasn't that *today* was
any finer in 1919 than in 1932," John Dos Passos explains, "it
was that in 1919 the tomorrows seemed vaster." Joseph Wood
Krutch in 1962 recalled what working for *The Nation* in the
Twenties had been like: "We were at bottom fundamentally
optimistic, and we were gay crusaders. . . . The future was
bright and the present was good fun at least." Nor is this only
a reminiscence of sometime literary radicals; after all, the period
dubbed itself the *New* Era, and the adjective carried the same
hopeful connotations it did when it qualified the words *Deal* and
Frontier, however different from one another may have seemed
the nouns.

"Given a chance to go forward with the policies of the last
eight years," Herbert Hoover declared on being nominated for
President in 1928, "we shall soon with the help of God be in
sight of the day when poverty will be banished from this nation"—although, as Frederick Lewis Allen pointed out, the candidate left one loophole in that acceptance speech: "It stipulated
that God must assist the Republican administration." But not
only Republicans and businessmen radiated optimism and con-
fidence, impressive as is the collection of just-before-the-deluge
pollyannisms uttered by bankers and stockbrokers which John
Kenneth Galbraith has lovingly recorded in *The Great Crash.*
The new social sciences also often expressed a prophetic vision
as sanguine as Hoover's. They saw a future in which all pain,
misery, and maladjustment would be seen as manifestations of
"culture-lag," a term first popularized in the Twenties; when the
lag caught up with the culture, presumably, all would be well.

In a provocative essay for the *American Political Science
Review,* "The Twentieth Century Enlightenment," Cushing
Strout in 1955 painted a composite picture which would have
fitted many a social theorist of the first third of this century, "contemptuous of the past, complacent about the present, and starry-

eyed before the future," with "a touching, if narrow, faith in the efficacy of science, to solve all problems and a passionate prejudice that his technical view of reason would promote progress." In the Twenties "the cause of progress was not moribund but merely catching its breath," writes Clarke Chambers; in spite of setbacks and frustrations "there persisted an unending search for new ways to meet problems both old and new." The social scientists and social workers commonly wanted the exact opposite of what a businessman of the period might have considered ideal, but John Dewey was in his own way as much a "booster" as anybody in the Chamber of Commerce. Charles A. Beard sensed the unintended cultural fellow-traveling here implied, and in the preface to a characteristic tract for the times, *Whither Mankind?* he declared that the problem for the would-be reformer in the Twenties was one of being optimistic without sounding like a real-estate salesman.

Looking at the same problem from an entirely different angle, in 1926 Hugo Gernsback founded *American Stories,* the first American magazine devoted entirely to science-fiction. (The second such journal came into being in 1929, and the third— the present-day *Analog,* which is trying to live down the fact that it began life as *Astounding Stories of Super Science*—was established in 1930.) And magazine science-fiction, as distinguished both from the consciously literary and from the horror-movie varieties, had in its pre-Hiroshima days a broad vein of propaganda for the Idea of Progress, with technological innovation and scientific discovery replacing Social Darwinism as history's motor-mechanism; significantly, Gernsback had published some of his first science-fiction in the pages of the *Electrical Experimenter*. An occasional practitioner like Howard Phillips Lovecraft might take a more Gothic tone, and the magazine *Weird Tales,* founded in 1923, in its own way shared in the literary disenchantments of the Twenties; but the phrase "brave new world" had not yet acquired the overtones Aldous Huxley was to give it in 1932, and a genre of popular fiction

B

which promised many a new thing under the sun seemed a fitting accompaniment to the new age of radio.

But the more one probes into attitudes toward Progress during the Twenties, the more these attitudes dissolve into ambivalence. Few spectacles were more ironic than that of Henry Ford, who was perhaps doing more to smash the old culture than any other single individual, at the same time rescuing selected relics of that culture—a Cape Cod windmill, a Mississippi paddle-wheel steamer—for the Greenfield Village museum he founded in the Twenties. This ambivalence as between the future and the past dogged Ford throughout his lifetime, and alongside the many paeans to Ford as a progressive innovator there was also, as Allan Nevins and Frank Ernest Hill acknowledged in the second volume of their history of the Ford Motor Company, a chorus of "liberals and intellectuals who made Ford the symbol of an all-potent industrialism trampling down individuality, beauty, and serenity and erecting machine-altars to Mammon and Moloch." One of the great German silent films, *Metropolis,* included a fantastic scene in which workers in a factory of the future who lagged behind its insensate pace were fed to the machines they served; it was no coincidence that the actor cast in the leading role for this picture bore a striking physical resemblance to Ford. Even in science-fiction, Prometheus the Fire-Bringer transmutes easily into Frankenstein.

Was the future bright with promise, or black with foreboding? "Lost" or otherwise, the generation of the Twenties had inherited a larger stock of ideas from the Gilded Age than it ordinarily cared to admit, and that stock had included other slogans besides those of complacent optimism. Vernon Louis Parrington, in one of the brilliant unfinished passages which make the third volume of his *Main Currents in American Thought* so tantalizing, characterized the intellectual climate of the allegedly gay Nineties as "The Darkening Skies of Letters"; the somber stoicism of men "left to wander . . . upon the bleak tablelands of impersonal energy," as Parrington put it, was as true a heritage from the later nineteenth century as was the humane progressivism of those whom Daniel Aaron has named the *Men of Good Hope,* and the tunes in a minor key which were learned on those "higher and bleaker tablelands of specu- lation" were played with great frequency during the Twenties.

These would be the Twenties of *The Waste Land,* of "All the Sad Young Men," and also of the sweated millhand and the disgruntled veteran—the generation which had found all the worst forebodings of its grandparents confirmed. Joseph Wood Krutch for example, even while enjoying life as a theater critic in New York, looked up from time to time at those darkening skies, and in 1929, at the existentially critical age of thirty-five, he distilled some of that darkness into an essay on *The Modern Temper.* Science, upon which some of his contemporaries pinned their hopes, could "not in any ultimate sense solve our problems," Krutch declared; on the contrary, "the more we learn of the laws of [the] universe . . . the less we shall feel at home in it." For modern man philosophy was a phantom, art no more than an opiate, tragic heroism a fallacy, and religion a lie. "We have grown used . . . to a Godless universe," he concluded one wintry chapter, "but we are not yet accustomed to one which is loveless as well, and only when we have so become shall we realize what atheism really means."

The Modern Temper, the present writer has found, still has power to break through the defenses of students against infection by a professor's ideas. But other classroom teachers have gotten a different response: "To us," said one typical undergraduate of the Sixties, "Mr. Krutch's pessimism seems quaint and rather sweet." Reacting to this comment, passed along to him by the student's instructor, the author of *The Modern Temper* gave himself the last word: "Since my own frame of mind is somewhat more cheerful in 1965 than it was in 1929, and since to be modern is to be much less cheerful than I was at my worst, regret at being dismissed is somewhat tempered by the realization that I could not be up-to-date without being thoroughly miserable."

But perhaps Krutch and the young disciple of "Sartre, Beckett, *et al.*" were both being unfair to the temper of the Twenties. Alongside the pessimism of elegiac resignation there was also a pessimism of dialectical action: destroy the sham hopes of the world we live in to make way for a better one. Vernon Louis Parrington, who carried into the Twenties the scars of older wars, wrote of "Sinclair Lewis: Our Own Diogenes" as just such a prophet of progress through deflation, rather than as the total misanthrope depicted by some of Lewis's other critics. Those merciless exposés of business fatuity and rural boorishness had the context of a posited utopia of science and rationality, which would "exalt the test-tube and deflate the cash register," dethrone the Babbitts and elevate the Arrowsmiths. So thought Parrington, then the dean of historians of American letters; and ever since that time the critics, in an argument best exemplified in the polemics of Frederick Hoffman and Bernard De Voto respectively, have debated whether the nay-saying intellectuals of the Twenties were engaged in destruction for the sake of creative innovation or were trapped in a comprehensive and pointless negativism.

The men of the Twenties might have been better able to answer that question for themselves had they possessed a better historical memory. We have already noted, at least by implication, that the chilling naturalistic vision of *The Modern Temper* was a distillate of troubled Victorian reflections on apes and angels; similarly, the idea of a revolutionary science of society so often put forth as "new" in the Twenties owed a great deal to the spadework in the Seventies and Eighties by American inquirers like Lewis H. Morgan, John Wesley Powell, and Lester F. Ward, and still earlier by European speculators such as Comte and Saint-Simon. Other liberations, constructive and otherwise, often associated with the Twenties as entirely new phenomena have been traced by Henry F. May to the "Greenwich Village" culture of the years before the First World War, and by Ray Ginger to the remarkable confluence of men, forces, and ideas in the Chicago of the Nineties. And the cultures of Chicago and New York and fading Boston in the Nineties or the Teens or the Twenties cannot be fully understood except in the context of Paris under the Republic of 1870, Berlin under Wilhelm I, and London in the old age of Queen Victoria.

But in the American Twenties, men evoked the past as an unreal abstraction, the conservatives tending to remember it as "good" (as in the slogan "back to Normalcy"), and the radicals to remember it as "bad" (for example, as "Puritanism"—see Hoffman's discussion of their misreading of this word). In neither case was there much awareness of the past's *congruity* with their own time and place, nor of the sources of supply for their own arsenals of ideas.

In the third volume of his all-but-forgotten *Cosmic Philosophy,* the would-be universal scholar John Fiske had declared: "Civilization runs in a definite path, [so] that the sum total of ideas and feelings dominant in the next generation will be the offspring of the sum total of ideas and feelings dominant in this." Commenting on that judgment toward the end of a series of lectures at Princeton in 1925, the physicist Louis Trenchard More remarked that if the statement were true it would "leave history forever as the great unattainable science." For "what is the sum total of ideas and feelings of a generation? If I examine myself, I am bewildered by the complexity and fugitiveness of my own ideas and feelings; those of my own generation are beyond my apprehension; and those of past generations fade into vacuity." Whatever this may amount to as a judgment about history in general—and it does sound rather like a gloss on Carl Becker's "Every man his own historian"— it is not a bad statement of the cultural climate of the Twenties, and it is a reminder that however much the period derived and borrowed from the times of John Fiske there were ways in which it sharply differed. This lack of a past included the lack of a revolutionary tradition to draw on, and without it the attempt to bring about a Great Liberation during the Twenties was inevitably crippled and impoverished. Van Wyck Brooks's famous polemic of 1920, *The Ordeal of Mark Twain,* scoring points off Grandpa instead of prudently investing his bequest of iconoclasm, is one of the more notorious examples.

The Great Liberation needed all the persuasive power it could muster, even including appeals to the past, for it was played out on a stage before an audience much of which was frightened, anti-intellectual, and reactionary. Tennessee wrote an anti-evolution law onto the books and kept it there until 1967 against all the big guns of metropolitan ridicule. Sacco and Vanzetti were debated, written about, rioted over, for seven years—and nevertheless executed. A weak Soviet Union, torn by famine and civil war, became enough of a bogeyman to alarm the United States in one of the most prosperous and secure periods in its entire history. The Ku Klux Klan stirred into new life in 1915 and grew strong enough to dictate policies and candidates as far away from its Southern home base as Indiana, Oregon, Kansas, and Maine. Intolerance, Paul L. Murphy sweepingly declared in 1964, "was an integral part of the 1920s, participated in consciously or unconsciously by the great majority of Americans," and "was specially suited to the peculiar culture and society of the jazz age."

Then what becomes of the familiar stereotype of the Revolt of Youth during the Twenties? Perhaps people like Van Wyck Brooks and Harold Stearns and the undergraduate subscribers to the *American Mercury* were talking primarily to one another. Abba Hillel Silver, a well-known American rabbi, contended in 1931 that the iconoclasm of the young had been "overplayed by middle-aged moralists and lecturers" during the preceding decade; that there was in fact "no more conservative, stand-pat young man in the world than the raccoon-coated 'homo sapiens' on the American campus"; and that "in matters that really count,

. . . in questions of social justice, war and peace," young Americans were "as orthodox, as unimaginative, and as submissive as the most hidebound Babbitts of their day." Their incidental bad manners might, from the standpoint of their elders, be revolting, but they did not constitute a revolt. And there were others whose judgment on reality was still more personal and private, such as the young women in college devoted primarily, in Rollene W. Saal's happy phrase, to "butterscotch sundaes, Yale boys, and Kahlil Gibran." *The Prophet* was first published in 1923, and became the most unexpected— that is, unpromoted—financial success in publishing history; it is indeed a curious book to account for as an integral part of the culture of the Jazz Age.

Arthur Schlesinger, Jr., has argued that the Twenties, far from having been a decade of flaming nonconformity, were in fact a period so gray that after such a stretch of dusty conservatism men would have gone out and made a New Deal, even without the stimulus of depression, out of sheer boredom. To be sure, throughout those years voices were heard advocating liberalism, progressivism, or socialism; but in his volume of the *Economic History of the United States,* dealing with the years 1917 to 1929, George Soule asserted that "the radical movements growing out of the war had been routed, and the ferment of opinion demanding economic reconstruction had almost disappeared." This may have been an exaggeration; yet twelve years after the publication of Soule's *Prosperity Decade,* Arthur Mann entitled his account of one doughty champion of reform causes during the Twenties *LaGuardia: A Fighter Against His Times.* And men of reforming intent who lacked the Little Flower's opportunity for responsible political life were usually more productive of inspired polemic than they were of programs for action.

Consider for example the surprising failure of the woman suffrage movement in its hour of triumph to fulfill either the hopes or the fears of Victorian and Progressive America. "The suffragists pardonably assumed that the revolution in women's status would constitute a social revolution," writes Aileen S. Kraditor, "but in fact the enfranchisement of women did not change the economic or political structure of American society." The new freedoms of the individual woman in the Twenties, at work but more conspicuously at play, still fell short of the promise, supposedly implicit in the Nineteenth Amendment, of a cleanup of American public life in general and of politics in particular. Indeed there seems to have been some degree of regression; so formidable a woman in public life as Belle Moskowitz, a major power in Al Smith's state administration at Albany, found it politic at a Columbia University forum in April, 1926, to declare her belief in the natural intellectual inferiority of women.

The choice of "Maw" Ferguson as governor of Texas in a fluke run-off primary in 1924 hardly qualifies as the exception that tests the rule; her husband had been impeached and removed from the same high office in 1917 and continued to call many of the plays in her administration, some of whose acts such as the censorship of schoolbooks for Texans bear comparison with the doings of the most Babbittish of her male political contemporaries. The reign of Mrs. Nellie Tayloe Ross as governor of Wyoming showed more promise, but did not signify the start of a trend. "Since the agitation for and the achievement of the franchise for women," Ida Clyde Clarke complained in a book published in 1925 with the provocative title *Uncle Sam Needs a Wife,* "he [Uncle Sam] has been courteously appointing us in negligible minorities on some of his advisory boards and commissions." Forty years later, American women would still be receiving token appointments in government or occasionally running for seats in Congress to succeed their deceased husbands—or in one notorious case, in Montgomery, Alabama, taking over a governor's mansion when her spouse's term of office expired in order to free him for concentration on higher things. To be sure, Lyndon B. Johnson, the arch-adversary of that particular husband-and-wife team, did champion the cause of further emancipation, and at the present writing had been successful in raising the political status of women in male American society about up to parity with that of Negroes.

The historical literature of the women's rights movement itself reflects this failure: a scattering of books and monographs by women, often dismissed by male historians with epithets like "feminist," and from most of the men a deafening silence. (In contrast, white historians *have* made many effective contributions to the history of the Negro rights movement.) As late as 1964 one such study, sociologist Jessie Bernard's *Academic Women,* had to be prefaced by testimonials from a leading male scholar in this woman author's own field and from her own academic dean (also, of course, male) to the effect that the book was free from axe-grinding or "female chauvinism"; it is rather as if a book by a pioneering Negro scholar had to be vouched for by two well-known white men in order to pass muster with a readership which could be presumed skeptical of the author's competence. The triumphant conversion of segregated men's bars into integrated speakeasies—later resegregated *de facto* at certain afternoon hours as cocktail lounges—scarcely suffices as compensation.

Switzerland, that bastion of European banking, continued by ballot of its male electorate to reject woman suffrage in the Sixties, and the contrast with the example of the Soviet Union— where no particular masculine mystique is attached to practicing medicine, operating construction machinery, or flying in outer space—reminds us of the old Marxist argument that full equality of the sexes would only be achieved under socialism; but the Twenties were scarcely a time to have attempted that solution for the United States. When Amory Blaine, in the closing pages of F. Scott Fitzgerald's *This Side of Paradise,* hitches a ride with a chauffeur-driven businessman and regales him with a vision of a socialist utopia, he is not even successful in being rude;

and one Fitzgerald biographer, Andrew Turnbull, has concluded that "Marxism . . . was fundamentally alien to Fitzgerald." Much that masqueraded as "radicalism" in the Twenties was radical only in the sense of *épater les bourgeois,* using a confusedly Marxist vocabulary for much the same reason that a later generation of student radicals would defend the use of four-letter words; "even in those with a strong impulse toward dissent," Richard Hofstadter has stated, "bohemianism triumphed over radicalism."

It was not *always* pure bohemianism. Joseph North's *Robert Minor: Artist and Crusader,* produced in 1956 under the imprimatur of American Communism's publication arm and as embarrassingly laudatory a biography as any company-sponsored sketch of the founder of a firm, nevertheless performed the worthwhile service of reprinting two dozen of Minor's sketches and cartoons, many of them dating from the Twenties. It is to be hoped that these savage, intensely human drawings will long outlive the shoddy cause of American Stalinism in which Minor was enlisted. One *Daily Worker* cartoon, for example, showed three pudgy figures representing American, British, and French imperialism surrounded by grinning armed giants labeled China, India, and Africa, with the caption "Who is that you all are going to whip, Mr. Legree?" In 1968 this carried if anything a more potent message than it had in 1925 —a message which, in the light of the tragedy of modern Asia, can hardly be shrugged off as "bohemian." And contrary to popular myth, James Weinstein writes, "relatively large numbers of trade unionists and farmers" in the Twenties were involved in a kind of politics "far to the left even of the LaFollette progressives," and in 1924 they "nearly succeeded in pulling together a genuinely national radical third party." But there was enough in the "radicalism" of the Twenties that was nihilistic, hedonistic, or merely naughty to give Hofstadter's comment considerable weight.

Of course, the bohemians had a point. In the pages of *The*

Liberator for December, 1920, Max Eastman warned: "The revolution will not come, or coming, it will not survive, if it depends fundamentally upon discipline." Twenty years later, in *Stalin's Russia and the Crisis in Socialism,* the former *Masses* editor elaborated: "The essential meaning of the revolution to me was the liberation of individuality, the extension of my privilege of individuality to the masses of mankind." Stalin's Russia by that time had made the idea of a disciplined socialism for the rest of the world even less attractive for Eastman than it had seemed in the Twenties: "For my own part I have not the glimmer of a desire to lose my identity in a collection, nor would I wish this loss upon a single workingman." This is not bohemianism, exactly; it calls to mind rather the Yankee Republicanism of Robert Frost, and before this impulse was spent it would carry Max Eastman still further to the Right.

John Dos Passos seems to have made much the same kind of pilgrimage from Left to Right—unless his present-day publisher is correct in saying that "the times themselves, rather than Dos Passos, have changed." In 1962 Daniel Aaron wrote of Dos Passos: "It is axiomatic with him that all institutions decay; the process accelerates as managers become separated more and more from the managed." "Organization is death," Dos Passos exclaimed in 1918, contemplating enlistment in the Army; and, deeply involved though he was in such "radical" causes of the Twenties as the Sacco-Vanzetti defense, in 1926 the novelist cautioned his friends on the Left as to what organization under the Communist Party might mean: "The terrible danger to explorers is that they always find what they are looking for." Reviewing a paperback reissue of *Three Soldiers* in 1965, Robie Macauley summed up the tragic individualism that linked the "leftist" novels of John Dos Passos in the Twenties and Thirties with his "rightist" essays of the Fifties and Sixties: "All the Davids of the earlier books . . . found an opportunity to organize, won their battles, and in the process turned into new Goliaths."

To be sure, as Daniel Aaron's *Writers on the Left* attests, the story did not always turn out quite that way. Much of the anarchic individualism of the Twenties, chastened by the experience of the Depression and by the recrudescence of international tyranny, was transformed in the early Thirties into a truly disciplined radical-socialist view of life; and Mr. Krutch was to find *The Nation* not so much fun to work for as his friends turned Communist, a process he watched in a frame of mind not unlike that of a civilized Roman pagan watching his friends turn Christian. Aaron and some of those writers themselves (for example, Granville Hicks in *Part of the Truth*, 1965, and Richard Wright in his essay for *The God That Failed*, 1950) have documented their discovery that the straitjacket of Marxism could be fully as galling as the bourgeois commercialism against which they had revolted in the first place.

The literary Stalinism of the Thirties, seen in retrospect as a heartfelt response to the challenge of depression and Fascism, retains a certain glamour, but seen from the standpoint of the Twenties, when it had been far more hazardous in America to be tarred as a "radical," the party-lining of the following decade becomes oddly unheroic. John Reed, torn by "the choice between loyalty to an ideal and loyalty to an organization" (if we may trust Theodore Draper's account of the last weeks of Reed's life in Russia), or the aged Eugene Debs telling the *Daily Worker* in 1924 that he was glad he had no "Vatican in Moscow" to guide him—such moments of truth give the latter-day Rightist taunts of Max Eastman and John Dos Passos considerable sting. But there is pathos in their recantations also. In 1964 Eastman, recalling almost wistfully a 1921 encounter with H. G. Wells, wrote: "There is—or was up to Lenin's time —a fraternity among all those who like to disturb the established inanities." The shift in verb tenses in that sentence from "is" to "was" measures with cruel accuracy the dilemma of radicalism in the twentieth century.

The dilemma had to be faced even by those among the free

spirits of the Twenties whose instincts were essentially Tory. Thus H. L. Mencken, ruminating on the state of the union two months before the 1920 election, confessed: "Though I am . . . in favor of property and would be quite content to see one mob of poor men (in uniform) set to gouging and hamstringing another mob of poor men (in overalls) in order to protect it, it by no means follows that I am in favor of the wealthy bounders who now run the United States." Should it come to a showdown between labor and capital in this country, Mencken predicted "a colossal victory for capitalism," which would "play off one mob against another, and pick the pockets of both"— but, the Baltimore sage ruefully added, "it will also pick *my* pockets."

After the Thirties, when Mencken not only supported Alf Landon for President but so suspended his newspaperman's intuition as to persuade himself that that gentleman could be elected, a theory gained currency that Mencken had "turned reactionary" in his later years. (Harvey Wish, for example, continued to suggest some such change in Mencken in the 1962 revision of his *Society and Thought in Modern America.*) Survivors of the Twenties could thus remember and cherish their favorite Mencken epigrams and still regretfully drop his post-1929 writings from the canon, except for a respectful bow toward *The American Language.* But in a still longer perspective it is becoming clear that the sage of Baltimore attacked FDR and Henry Wallace on much the same grounds that he had attacked the political leaders of the Twenties, if with somewhat more bitterness and somewhat less flair. The contemporary social scene, rather than Mencken, had changed—one no longer won applause by referring to the mental processes of the working class as "a kind of insensate sweating, like that of a kidney" —and the foreign context had changed even more. Mencken's admiration of Nietzsche, Bavarian beer, and by extension all things German got by in the Twenties because all Americans were presumably disillusioned with "the archangel Woodrow's" crusade to end war by downing the Hun; but during the Thirties and Forties the term "pro-German" came, in many American minds, automatically to mean "pro-Nazi," and Mencken's laughter at the *Untermenschen* (as he viewed them) seemed to have a more sinister ring.

Still, Mencken in his great days had been admired for his opposition to many of the things the radicals of his generation also disliked: religion, Prohibition, Victorianism, commercialism, stupidity, and fraud; indeed, the fact that he and they disliked so many of the same things may have helped to keep his memory green for a newer generation of American intellectuals recoiling from what they have variously called "mass culture," *"kitsch,"* or "ticky-tacky," in much the same frame of mind in which Mencken had recoiled from, or rather jeered at, similar manifestations of American life in the Twenties. His jibes at the New Deal forgotten if not forgiven, essays from the Twenties like "Valentino," "The Sahara of the Bozart," and "The Libido for the Ugly" (with its anticipation of modern discussions of urban sprawl) once again seemed as lively and relevant as they had to any reader of the *American Mercury*. To be sure, Mencken's anti-Babbittism had been uttered from a vantage point above Babbitt, as it were—that is, a vantage point not of underdog opposition but of aristocratic disdain—but perhaps this frankly aristocratic bias has helped to give these old essays their verve and bite as compared with the outpourings of some of the more recent culture-critics, unable to reconcile an essentially elitist aesthetic with their own mildly liberal (sometimes pronounced "radical") political preconceptions.

It is one of the charms and pitfalls of the Twenties that elements in them which a present consensus had decided were dated and quaint have a way of suddenly coming to seem contemporary and familiar; these Mencken essays are only one example. If this is true of the "high culture" of that decade it is even more true of what might be called the "low"—the newspaper sensations, the publicizing of inconsequential personalities and events, or as Carey McWilliams once put it, "the pervading nonsense, cynicism, credulity, speakeasy wit, passion for debunkery, sex-craziness, and music-hall pornography of the times." Part of the enduring charm, and classroom utility, of Frederick Lewis Allen's *Only Yesterday* can be attributed to the fact that much of what Allen captured in 1931 before it had frozen into "history" still strikes many readers as fresh and alive. We turn his pages on the great court trials, on the public discussion of the revolution in morals, or on the Florida real-estate boom, and we feel that we know where we are.

Allen's book scores some of its strongest recognition-points with readers both old and young when it dwells upon the development of athletic competitions into national mass entertainment. There is a marked contrast between the world symbolized in the pre-World War I society-page treatment of Ivy League football and in Theodore Roosevelt's little moral homilies based on sports ("Don't foul, and don't shirk, and hit the line hard"), on the one hand, and the elaborate apparatus of build-up, commercial tie-ins, and harmless nonsense surrounding a latter-day championship fight or bowl game, on the other. From something accessible only to an immediate local audience (except at second-hand by way of telegraphed reports to the newspapers), fun and games became national in an altogether new way in the Twenties thanks to the development of radio broadcasting, and have remained so ever since; the difference between the arena erected for the Jack Dempsey–Tom Gibbons fight in 1923, whose ruins remain on Montana's "high line" near Shelby to prompt philosophic reflection, and the laughably ill-executed shelter erected for the Houston Astros in 1965 is one only of degree, not of kind.

Paul Gallico's sketches of the sporting figures of the Twenties (Bobby Jones, Bill Tilden, Dempsey, Red Grange, Babe Ruth, and others), widely syndicated on newspaper sports pages in 1964, made it plain that at least one aspect of those years still commanded a sense of psychic contemporaneity among a great many Americans. It all seemed so familiar—even the scandals, such as the 1919 "Black Sox," were to have echoes in boxing and in college football and basketball in later years—that the reader in a world changing even more rapidly than that of the Twenties clung to what by a fine irony had come to seem relatively timeless; two- and three-platoon systems and the "lively ball" to the contrary notwithstanding, the rules and stratagems and (especially) little rituals had not changed as much as had the rules and stratagems of politics, business, and war. It may be a sign of a certain left-handed sanity in the national psyche that an American soldier, captured by the Communists in the first tense summer of the Korean War and then liberated in a counterattack by United Nations forces, brushed aside all ideological questions in his first press interview and impatiently asked, "Are the Phillies still in first place?"

But this suggests that Carey McWilliams's blast at the Twenties as "a period that invested the trivial with a special halo" may have been unduly harsh; better the trivial than the hysterical, perhaps. Robert K. Murray has argued that the shift of public attention in the spring of 1920 "from the antics of Lusk and Palmer to those of Dempsey and Babe Ruth" may have done more to abate the madness of the Great Red Scare of 1919 than any reasoned arguments for freedom of speech, and thus it may not have been altogether a bad thing that the newspapers of the period "began to view American life not so much as a political and economic struggle but as a hilarious merry-go-round of sport, crime, and sex." Heywood Broun caught this change of mood in a fanciful essay for *The Nation,* in which he imagined the hellfire preacher John Roach Straton journeying to heaven on a hot July afternoon in 1920 to ask that fire be rained on Manhattan because forty thousand people were watching Sunday baseball in Yankee Stadium; and then, Broun reported, as Babe Ruth came up to the plate God replied to Straton, "Let's at least wait until the inning's over."

However, if the world of spectator sport during the Twen-

ties seems reassuringly familiar to the modern reader, this is
not as true of other forms of mass entertainment. The present
writer has observed, for example, the discomfort of a modern
audience at a full-length screening, with no dubbed sound-
track, of the elder Douglas Fairbanks's version of *The Thief
of Bagdad*; the trouble with the classics of the silent screen,
for people conditioned by a more noisy, "talky" culture even
than that of the Twenties, is that they *are* silent. In spite of
this particular film's ingenious and imaginative sets, striking
as spectacle even by post-wide-screen standards, the audience
—incidentally, a metropolitan university "foreign film" crowd
—literally could not take it sitting down. *Something* comes
across, the crucial test being that small children, innocent of
the critical moviegoer's intellectual conditioning, continue to
get the message of Chaplin or the Keystone Cops or Harold
Lloyd, but otherwise most of the motion pictures of the Twenties seem to bring us psychically closer to the era of the gas-
light and the cigar-store Indian.

As for the legitimate stage, the Twenties have been all
but unanimously hailed as the greatest, if not the only, flowering
of the theater in America, whereas the Forties and Fifties were
conspicuously marked by notices, perhaps premature, of that
medium's impending death. Indeed, if theater since the Second
World War seems to have had difficulty finding itself, with the
significant exception of the musical, part of the trouble may be
that the theater of the Twenties did its work too well. Any
artistic development poses the problem to its successors: "Can
you top this?" If the stage of the Jazz Age asserted freedom for
normal sex (see Chapters IV–VIII of W. David Sievers, *Freud
on Broadway,* 1955), then there was nothing left along this
line for a later generation to assert except freedom for *psy-
chopathia sexualis;* if Eugene O'Neill set his broodingly nihilistic philosophy in a traditional, even formalistic play-structure,
thereby giving it the disciplined tension that helped to make it
"good theater," then by the Fifties it would become necessary

c

to extend nihilism to the structure itself, so that it was not always clear that audiences were viewing plays at all. The Theater of the Absurd does have important roots in the Twenties (some work of the Provincetown group; the Dadaist circle in Paris; Brecht in Germany), but on the whole, when one compares *What Price Glory?* or even *Strange Interlude* with, say, *Waiting for Godot,* or in a different vein the agonies of Tennessee Williams, the Broadway of the Twenties seems relatively homey and old-fashioned.

What about jazz as an element of congruity between past and present? It is older than the Twenties, of course, and most white Americans know by now that the only reason the period qualifies as *the* Jazz Age is that it was the time when middle-class Mr. Charlie "discovered" this musical idiom. Gilbert Osofsky in an article for the *American Quarterly* has set this encounter in a wider historical context, within which the white man is perennially discovering a "new" Negro, in the case of the Twenties inventing a fantasy of Harlem as Happytown to serve a function for America akin to that traditionally provided by Paris—a fantasy that Repeal and Depression would quickly dispel. For jazz in particular, the irony here is that militant Negroes seem to have rejected identification with that form of music for the very reason that some whites accepted the medium; that it was manifestly a folk, even a popular, art and was thus "lowbrow."

In another *American Quarterly* article, Chadwick Hansen documents the fact that the Chicago *Defender* during the Twenties invertedly accepted the white South's stereotype of jazz as "nigger music" and therefore attacked it as something Negroes must live down. Dave Peyton, a columnist for that crusading Negro newspaper, wrote hopefully in 1928 that "jazz is on the wane." As for the white intelligentsia, jazz at the outset had little more prestige among them than, for example, Twist music (as music) had in the early Sixties, for all the valiant effort of Gilbert Seldes in *The Seven Lively Arts* (1924) to persuade them otherwise.

There were exceptions, such as the premiere of the semi-jazz *Rhapsody in Blue* at Aeolian Hall in New York and the recognition by Serge Koussevitsky, the elegant conductor of the Boston Symphony, that "jazz is an important contribution to modern musical literature"; and there were efforts at didactic praise such as the five paragraphs on jazz in the Beards' *Rise of American Civilization* (1927). But there persisted for years a sense of its antithesis to all "longhair" music, and correspondingly a rejection of what was called "jazz" (loosely grouped with the society dance-orchestra, radio, and popular sheet-music) by professed devotees of "good," that is, classical, music. Sinclair Lewis made the most benighted of his characters (in *The Man Who Knew Coolidge,* for example) enjoy jazz as a symptom of their Babbittry, and even F. Scott Fitzgerald, it seems to this reader, was slumming a bit in his references to the medium.

In the journals of news and opinion, one characteristic comment was that of Paul Poiret, a Paris fashion designer, in the *Forum* for January, 1927. Quite unlike the Frenchman of the Fifties, with his taste for *le jazz hot,* M. Poiret recoiled in civilized horror from "the implacable and hypertrophic rhythms of the new dances, the blues and the Charlestons, the din of unearthly instruments, and the musical idioms of exotic lands." He predicted that "the thrall of American music, which with Paul Whiteman [!] seems to have reached its paroxysm and its zenith, will die away," and become one with "the gypsy rhythms which now seem so naïve and old-fashioned to us." The jazz of the Twenties may indeed have sounded naïve and old-fashioned to rock-'n'-roll-attuned ears in the Sixties; but who, apart from the most specialized of ethno-musicologists, was studying gypsy music with the same reverent intensity that its devotees brought to Dixieland?

A time was coming when the tables would be turned, when the undergraduate music major would compose in a jazz idiom with the approval of his major professors, and the jazz critic, as serious in his musical purpose as Bernard Shaw and Berlioz had been in their critical essays, would become a fixture in magazines read by intellectuals. And the inevitable happened. "The advanced jazzmen," writes Wilfrid Mellers, "began to emulate the advanced straight musicians of a slightly earlier generation: they deplored the philistinism of their public, and played for themselves and their initiates." For these men too the older jazz came to be "despised as 'Jim Crow music'; and the advanced jazzmen began to . . . distinguish themselves as an elite." Meanwhile the popular culture, and the commercial media with which it is in perpetual if uneasy alliance, had recoiled against jazz as being too complex, dowdy, and intellectual. Reaching into the "rhythm-and-blues" subsoil whence jazz itself had come, between them these forces invented rock-'n'-roll. By the Fifties we had come full circle; a university dean who had learned a good deal about jazz in a conscientious effort to swing with the younger generation was loftily informed by his own teenaged daughter that jazz was strictly for squares.

How far the jazz musicians and their hearers had come since the Twenties may be gauged from an incident in 1964 when San Francisco's Jazz Workshop, in order to keep an engagement with advanced jazzman Miles Davis without violating California law (Davis's new percussionist being not yet twenty-one), surrendered its liquor license for two weeks, served soft drinks for inflated prices, and packed the house to the doors. The jazz setting of the era of Izzie and Moe—the smoky speakeasy, illegal by definition—had been an altogether different world. When Leopold Stokowski predicted around 1925 that jazz was destined to "have the same revivifying effect as the injection of new, and in the larger sense, vulgar blood into dying aristocracy," it is rather doubtful that this fashionably-dressed jazz audience of the Sixties, quaffing Coca-Cola or Seven-Up and politely listening (not dancing) to Mr. Davis's music, was quite what that dynamic longhair musician had had in mind; but at least, unlike the uptown slummers of the Twenties, this latter-day crowd was racially integrated.

Professional sports, the movies, the theater, jazz. Has our emphasis been undue, for an essay destined to be employed in work-haunted Academia? In a cryptic headnote for his anthology *The Twenties: Fords, Flappers, and Fanatics*—a far better compendium than the come-on title suggests—George E. Mowry wrote: "The vast crowds that attended the sporting events of the Twenties were probably responding to something deeper than to the blandishments of the professional pitchmen." In his preface, Mowry atoned for his title by taking issue with superficial, "era-of-wonderful-nonsense" interpretations and argued that we should take the decade far more seriously than has been the custom of historians, intimating "that the Twenties were really the formative years of modern American society." Mowry's first statement might be taken as a clue to the meaning of his second. And a quietly influential article by Leo Lowenthal, which first appeared in 1944 in a volume with the unpromising title *Radio Research,* has given us some insight into what the "something deeper" may have been.

Lowenthal made an intensive and imaginative study of the short, fact-studded, journalistic biographies of persons in public life to be found in the pages of the *Saturday Evening Post* and, before its untimely demise in 1957, *Collier's*. He tabulated these biographical essays for sixteen sample years ranging between 1901 and 1941, on the hypothesis that any marked and consistent changes in subject matter and treatment might be diagnostic of change in the nature of American popular ideals, and thus perhaps of the national character. His findings, for so modest an undertaking, were rather startling. Lowenthal's article contained in germ many of the theories of social change in America which were to be put forth in the Fifties: change from an "inner-directed" to an "other-directed" character in society; from an "old," "free professional" to a "new," "bureaucratized" middle class; from a "Protestant Ethic" to a "Social Ethic," or to a "fun morality"; from a society based on an economics of scarcity to an "affluent society"; and from an aesthetic polarized between "high" and "low" cultures to a bland "Midcult" that threatens to swallow both. More limited in what it overtly describes than most of these later studies, the Lowenthal monograph is even more sweeping in what it implies, and the present writer therefore digests it here without further apology.

In the first place, in Lowenthal's earliest sample (for the year 1901) the subjects of these popular biographical articles were overwhelmingly people who had achieved success in workaday or enterprising ways: the immigrant scientist, the industrial or financial leader, the serious artist or writer, the prominent candidate for high office. By 1941, the proportion of essays on such persons had declined sharply; as a matter of fact, since the scientists and businessmen and statesmen in the last of the samples tended to be marginal or bizarre—for example, Ponzi, the fraudulent financier, and Dr. Brinkley, the goatgland specialist—one might say that the percentage had shrunk to insignificance. Meanwhile, the representatives men held up to the attention of a mass audience had come to consist overwhelmingly of professional athletes and people from the entertainment world—ballplayers, stars and starlets, boxers, a sideshow barker, and a gorilla named Toto. Lowenthal called his earlier batch of biographical subjects "idols of production" and his later sample "idols of consumption," inferring from these categories a major transformation of American national aspirations. However devoted to "initiative," "rugged individualism," and productive enterprise our public rhetoric remained in theory, in the imaginative world of these biographies "the real battlefield of history recedes from view or becomes a stock backdrop while society disintegrates into an amorphous crowd of consumers."

Moreover, Lowenthal argued, in addition to holding up idols of consumption rather than of production for attention and superlative esteem, the authors of such articles had drastically changed their conception of how their subjects got to the top. The life-history of the hero at the turn of the century had been modeled on the myth of the self-made man, well within the Benjamin Franklin, Horatio Alger, log-cabin-to-presidency tradition: an individual, born and reared in obscurity or under hardship (for example, Theodore Roosevelt's asthma, George Washington Carver's race), strives toward success and, through qualities of his own character—strength, skill, intelligence, courage, or painstaking thoroughness—in due course achieves his goal. But the hero of the Aspirin Age, said his magazine biographers, underwent a quite different life experience: growing up sometimes in comparable oblivion, he often suffers comparable hardships, but then gets a break. (The talent scout happens to change a travel itinerary and by chance discovers the person he is looking for, et cetera.) Success for these people is not something they achieve, but something that *happens* to them, through forces as far beyond their control as earthquake or flood: "the success of our heroes of consumption is itself goods of consumption."

Consequently, the heroes of this consumer society are no longer held up as models for imitation by the reader; "there is no road left to him for an identification with the great, or for an attempt to emulate their success." No road, that is, except the palliative of identifying with them as fellow consumers. And so the biographers painstakingly note that for all their fame and fortune these public figures use the same kind of toothpaste or deodorant that John Doe does. The reader's distance from the hero's dizzying heights is bridged not by implicit admonition to go and do likewise but by the comforting reminder that in little ways we are all alike.

One could argue of course that this newer way of treating public or private lives was simply an echo in popular biography of the greater realism which had long been coming into serious literature. The real world of the nineteenth century had after all been a world whose successful few, not whose unsuccessful many, had fashioned its myths. Lowenthal does concede that the mass society of the twentieth century may be more accurately described as it has been by these magazine biographers, as a busy-work world of pointless small sufferings and satisfactions punctuated occasionally for elect individuals by "the breaks," than it could ever have been portrayed in a literature of emulation. But the abandonment of an ideal, even if it be illusory, can have profound behavioral consequences; even Marx and Engels, one must remember, had argued that a shift in the ideological superstructure of society can dialectically interact with the base.

At the same time, that concrete material base of society does remain decisive, and not only for Marxists: "Man does not live by bread alone," Norman Thomas once preached, "but he does live by bread." For this very reason the Lowenthal thesis, derived from a change wholly within the superstructure of ideology which nevertheless parallels a change within the base (that is, from an economy organized around primary production to an economy geared to mass-consumption), seems to the present writer so extraordinarily persuasive: it satisfies one's lust for philosophical concreteness without falling into the Marxist or counter-Marxist view that the world we live in is somehow somebody's "fault." It is worth noting that the editorial biases of the *Saturday Evening Post* in particular for most of the period studied by Lowenthal were those of George Horace Lorimer, an unreconstructed Old Guard Republican who never abandoned the Horatio Alger mystique in his editorials; thus, any change in the magazine's contents would seem attributable more to real changes in the magazine purchasers' own values than to changes in what Lorimer wanted them to believe.

"The modern individual seems subjected to decisive trends," Lowenthal wrote in summation, under the influence of which "he appears no longer as a center of outwardly bound energies and actions, . . . no longer as an integral unity on whose work and efficiency might depend not only his kin's future and happiness, but at the same time, mankind's progress in general"; instead, modern man's new heroes represent "a craving for having and taking things for granted . . . for a phantasmagoria of world-wide social security . . . for an attitude which has lost any primary interest in how to invent, shape, or apply the tools leading to such purposes of mass satisfaction." That may be pushing the hypothesis further than its data warrant, but should this little study of biographies in popular magazines in fact be diagnostic of the American condition, then the Twenties, with their outpouring of new kinds of consumer goods, their declining industrial labor force which nevertheless was able to produce more of those goods, their standardization and promotion of marketing by means of national mass advertising, and their critical but confused intellectual class, would be crucial for understanding so drastic a change.

Here and there in the record are clues pointing in that direction. Robert and Helen Lynd's classic *Middletown* takes on new meaning when read in the light of the Lowenthal thesis; even the statistics are there for comparison (Table XXIV). And Richard Hofstadter has noted that, while the angry young men of the Twenties continued the attacks on businessmen which had been a favorite sport of their Progressive predecessors, the character of the target had subtly altered: "Where the writers of the Progressive era had attacked the businessman for his economic and political role, the intellectuals of the twenties . . . assailed him for his personal and cultural incapacities. Where once he had been speculator, exploiter, corrupter, and tyrant, he had now become boob and philistine, prude and conformist, to be dismissed with disdain." Was this shift in rhetoric an acceptance of the "hard fact" of prosperity, as Hofstadter implies? Or was it a dim recognition of what Thorstein Veblen had proclaimed long before, namely that this misnamed "captain of industry" was as much the passive (if conspicuous) consumer as any of the people whom he, through the System, exploited?

Obviously, the Twenties remained a period of unabashed admiration for the idols of production, or at least of exchange. Singling out one such "rich, powerful, self-made giant," the electric utilities leader Samuel Insull, Forrest McDonald asserts that "in the hero-worshipping postwar decade, Insull became the Babe Ruth, the Jack Dempsey, the Red Grange of the business world." But this particular choice of metaphors suggests that the timbre of the praise of businessmen, like that of blame as noted by Hofstadter, had already begun to change: "His doings, small and large, became a great spectator sport, and they were reported and followed accordingly." Even so strongly "production"-oriented a study of a figure of the Twenties as is McDonald's *Insull* thus can lead one back to Lowenthal's "amorphous crowd of consumers"; indeed, elsewhere in the volume McDonald calls Insull "the crucial link between Phineas T. Barnum and Madison Avenue," which would seem to vitiate the case for his hero as an idol of production.

Moreover the producers themselves in the Twenties were becoming more aware of the consumer. Joseph Dorfman cites one 1927 estimate that advertising expenditures amounted to one and a half billion, an increase of 50 per cent over 1921, and quotes Julius Klein, director of the Bureau of Foreign and Domestic Commerce, in 1928: "The world as a whole is still obviously in its earliest experimental stages with installment selling, with such mass distributive apparatus as chain stores and mail-order establishments, and with problems of more accurate market-appraisal estimates of potential buying power, etc." Going into debt for consumer purchases, a practice condemned in previous more frugal eras as the last refuge of the spendthrift incompetent, came to be honored as a way to raise the standard of living and stave off depression—although in 1926 one Farmer-Laborite radical objected: "The people have mortgaged their future to live in the present. Even opium would not enable a man to invent a system of that kind."

Not only cosmetics and kilowatts, but ideas also, as the perennially observant Walter Lippmann reported in 1922, were increasingly being packaged into marketable "stereotypes" for mass consumption—and, one might metaphorically add, paid for on the installment plan. "We are told about the world before we see it," Lippmann wrote; and, fatalistically, "The way in which the world is imagined determines at any particular moment what men will do." Of course the Lowenthal thesis itself could easily become just such a stereotype as Lippmann described, and like any other hypothesis it ought to be dropped at once should it cease to explain facts and begin to explain them away. But applied to the Twenties, this hypothesis (or stereotype) is richly suggestive. The superficial froth of the period may have been sprayed forth from some deep and terrifying ocean currents indeed.

The life and liberty and property and happiness of the common man throughout the world are at the absolute mercy of a
few persons whom he has never seen, involved in complicated
quarrels that he has never heard of.

GILBERT MURRAY, *The League of Nations
and the Democratic Idea* (1921)

You just do it. Instinctively. You don't think. Your man is
there and you hit him with the ball.

Y. A. TITTLE, quoted in *The New York Times* (1964)

TWO

Of Coolidge and Hemingway

At 2:39 P.M., Dallas time, on November 22, 1963, on board
the Air Force jet which earlier that day had carried John F.
Kennedy toward his rendezvous with death, Lyndon Baines
Johnson took the oath of office as President of the United
States. The old words prescribed in the Constitution had the
whine of engines for accompaniment, and the new leader gave his
first order as President in the laconic language of the New
Frontier: "Now, let's get airborne." The contrast with the one
such transfer of power which took place during the Twenties
is startling: the country justice of the peace, John C. Coolidge,

34

lighting a kerosene lamp in the living room of the family farm-house in Plymouth, Vermont, to administer the oath of office to his son, who happened to be home on vacation.

As Vice-President, Calvin Coolidge had been a product of one of the touching democratic accidents that can befall even the best managed of national nominating conventions. "Com-pletely dominated by sinister predatory economic forces" as was the Republican convention of 1920 (in the judgment of the Kansas newsman William Allen White, who had covered every Republican presidential nomination since McKinley's), it was not so utterly prostrate as to grant those interests' every wish; having swallowed Warren Harding for President, it gagged on Irvine Lenroot, the senatorial cabal's choice for Vice-President, and instead rose in rebellion to nominate Coolidge. But his subsequent elevation to the chief magistracy, William Leuchten-burg has suggested, turned out to be a blessing in disguise for the economic masters of his party, whose luster had begun to be dimmed by the mounting scandals of the Harding Administra-tion. "Coolidge came along at a fortuitous time, just when the democratic creed was in need of a new version of an old symbol," writes Leuchtenburg, and, once the decks of the Ship of State had been cleared of Warren Harding's jolly pirate crew, the new President "served the needs of big business and the Old Guard even better than Harding had."

But to phrase his Presidency as merely having served the needs of the predatory interests is a bit unfair to Coolidge; the New Englander's political style also appears to have been con-genial to the public at large. Faced with a major coal strike in the opening days of his administration, Coolidge yielded the initiative in settling it to Governor Gifford Pinchot of Penn-sylvania, feeling that "dynamic federal action would usurp the state's functions." Pinchot's progressive Republican ad-mirers saw in his successful strike settlement the germ of a chance to wrest the GOP nomination in 1924 away from the Presi-dent. All that happened, however, was that the Pennsylvania

Governor got the blame for the resulting increase in the price of coal! "Although the problems of the day called for foresight and boldness," Robert H. Zieger concludes, "politics called for caution and inertia; Coolidge had triumphed by doing nothing."

Of course, there *were* voices calling for foresight and boldness in dealing with the problems of the day, but in a period like the 1920's, Francis L. Broderick writes, "the creative squad of liberal reformers bustle and plot amazing conferences and committee meetings at which the like-minded ignore facts, smile bravely, and build for the future"—and when the polls are closed they just don't have the votes. On Election Day of 1924 the voters, faced with the choice either of a candidate almost as conservative in John W. Davis, the honest corporation counsel whom the Democrats after 103 agonized ballots had chosen to represent them that year, or of a "radical" third-party nominee, gave the Yankee incumbent a full four-year term in his own right. Such, at any rate, seemed to be the sentiments of those who bothered; on August 17 the venerable Springfield *Republican* complained: "There are several million people who are more interested in the big league championship races than in the differences of opinion of Calvin Coolidge, John W. Davis, and Robert M. LaFollette."

To be sure, when the Democratic Party assembled for its marathon in Madison Square Garden, as John D. Hicks notes, "ten plays on Broadway had to close during the convention for lack of business." But all that this proved was that politics was a better drawing card—which, if the Lowenthal thesis has any relevance for the Twenties, is only what one might expect. Contemporary advertisements for radio receivers exploited the development of politics into a mass spectator sport: "Cheer with the galleries when the delegates march in! . . . Hear the pros and cons as they fight their way to a platform for you!" To some degree this process was disguised as greater participation ("It used to be all for the delegates' wives and the 'big' folks of politics. Now it's for everybody."), but RCA did not claim that the cheers uttered in one's home beside the Radiola were going to affect the outcome.

This early example of the "hard sell" should remind us also that the national economy in the Twenties had largely ceased to be of a kind which would have accorded with Calvin Coolidge's thrifty Yankee ideals. While the President was lecturing his press conference on the need for business and political leaders to keep in mind "the point of view of the great bulk of citizens of the country," whom Coolidge visualized in pastoral terms as "mainly responsible for keeping their houses, farms and shops in repair and maintaining them as a going concern," a thousand other voices, from the stockbroker wooing the investor to the advertiser wooing the housewife, were drowning out the traditional cautions of "Waste not, want not" and "Save for a rainy day." Historians began noticing this phenomenon early in the game: "Huge areas of American social power were now occupied by huckstering shock troops," Charles and Mary Beard wrote in 1927, and these "embattled vendors" rose to new heights of respectability and sovereignty even as they "pushed goods, desirable and noxious alike, upon a docile herd that took its codes from big type and colored plates." There is economic as well as moral meaning in William Allen White's choice of title for his biography of Calvin Coolidge, *A Puritan in Babylon:* The Yankee small-town boy, scion of the old production-oriented economy, was in effect presiding over its liquidation.

It used to be assumed that Coolidge was essentially a passive observer of this historical process rather than an active participant in it. The President uttered a few clipped New England aphorisms, always good for spicing an otherwise dull American history lecture on the politics of the Twenties; he vetoed a number of constructive measures proposed by the progressive rearguard which still survived in Congress; he labored diligently to retire the debt, balance the budget, cut down on government functions ("getting rid of our war activities" was one of the ways he put this); and otherwise, apart from a few pleats and tucks here and there such as the tariff and the air-mail subsidies, his administration was content to let the Roaring Twenties roar on. "We never paid any attention to what the books said about Harding and Coolidge," a former co-ed reminisces, "because we knew the professors were in a hurry to get to Roosevelt, and the term paper was going to be on the New Deal." A just criticism, as Howard Quint acknowledged in 1964 in a lecture attended by the present writer: "We know more about the Socialists and Communists in the 1920's than we do about the Republicans."

We know a little more about one of the Republicans since Quint and Robert H. Ferrell unearthed the typescript of President Coolidge's press conferences (in a wooden box which had been shipped to the public library of Coolidge's home city of Northampton, Massachusetts, at the end of his second term as President, and forgotten). "You do find in Coolidge an essential dignity," says Professor Quint, who takes exception to the old stereotype (as in Irving Stone's sketch of Coolidge for *The Aspirin Age*) in which the President's reserve and shyness were confused with lack of feeling; and one of the surviving members of the Coolidge press corps confessed to these new editors, "We kinda liked the old coot." In the privacy of the press conferences "silent" Calvin Coolidge opened up to such an extent that Quint and Ferrell entitled their edited selections from the transcript of those conferences *The Talkative President;* and this garrulous Yankee (when he chose to be) turns out to have been far more skillful as a politician and more believable as a human being than the cracker-barrel caricature who has appeared in lectures and textbooks for quite some time now. The Beards, who tried to puncture the "silence" myth in Coolidge's own lifetime ("Coolidge was in truth a facile and versatile speaker and writer," and more to the same effect), gave us a lead here which has usually been ignored.

For one thing, Coolidge appears to have used these press

conferences as an instrument for shaping public opinion, fully as consciously as Franklin Roosevelt or John Kennedy used theirs. They were not the joyous fencing-matches, nor the brilliant, briefed-to-the-eyebrows performances, which the latter two Presidents respectively enjoyed, but they did enable Coolidge to secure skillful and sympathetic accounts of his administration —better ones, as he confessed to the reporters, than he could have composed himself. Moreover, Quint and Ferrell assert, in his answers to the newsmen's questions, "the President ranged over a wide variety of subjects with a degree of expertise that historians of a later generation not always have appreciated." To be sure, his remarks "reflected a way of looking at government and politics that is completely out of fashion today"; but when Coolidge turned his attention to the merits of a particular measure before the Congress, say these editors, "his analysis of the issues could be penetrating," and whether or not in retrospect one agrees with his judgment on an issue, the talkative President often showed the "mastery over detail that every truly successful politician must possess."

Was the man more than a mere political technician? The student must answer that question from these records for himself. Was he no more than an apologist for big-business domination? On April 10, 1928, discussing a flood-control bill then pending in Congress, Coolidge expressed a worry that the people and property in need of protection in the flood zone had been lost sight of: "It has become a scramble to take care of the rail-roads and the banks and the individuals that may have invested in levee bonds, and the great lumber concerns that own many thousands of acres in that locality." A month later, in the pages of *The New Republic,* Rexford Tugwell would argue that "the stronghold of Jeffersonianism has shifted from the South to the Northeast and that its latter-day prophet is Coolidge"; but the foregoing and other lines from the presidential press conferences of the man from Vermont carry also at least a faint echo from the Age of Jackson.

D

It is faint indeed, compared with the color and fire of the Progressive minority that fought him from the other end of Pennsylvania Avenue—if indeed it *was* a minority; Arthur Link has reminded us that "various progressive coalitions controlled Congress for the greater part of the 1920's and were always a serious threat to the conservative administrations that controlled the executive branch." But if Coolidge's character and opinions were anachronistic in the Twenties, to a great extent so were theirs. The LaFollette presidential candidacy in 1924 is a case in point. Veterans of the Bull Moose campaign and even of Populism gathered under the Progressive banner, and William Leuchtenburg quotes a LaFollette leader as having said afterward that they ought to have campaigned to the tune of "Tenting Tonight on the Old Camp Ground." When one reflects further that much of the voting strength which rallied behind Old Bob seems to have been Irish and German-American, retroactive approval of his opposition to the 1917 declaration of war, a vote much of which Samuel Lubell has shown "actually had nothing to do with liberalism," one is forced to the conclusion that not only Calvin Coolidge but many of his opponents were also Puritans in Babylon.

One recent trend in the historical interpretation of these rebels on Capitol Hill has indeed been to treat them as throwbacks to the Progressive Era, or earlier, rather than as harbingers of the New Deal (Fiorello LaGuardia and perhaps George Norris excepted). Marian C. McKenna's admiring biography of the "sagebrush diplomat" William E. Borah stressed his "devotion to the older America," and presented the Idaho senator's "progressivism" in language more appropriate to the Old Frontier than to the New: "Reverencing the political system of simpler days, he had no desire to multiply agencies and institutions, make life more complicated, and pile new bureaucracies on old ones." These are words not so very different from those of Calvin Coolidge, telling his private press conference, "We have got so many regulatory laws already that in general I feel that we would be just as well off if we didn't have any more."

Robert LaFollette's running mate in 1924, Burton K. Wheeler, illustrates the point still more dramatically. Gadfly enough to have been called "Bolshevik Burt" by the kept press of his home state, and a strenuous prosecutor (and victim!) of the Harding cronies, by a twist of fate Wheeler one day would become the floor leader of the Senate opposition to Franklin Roosevelt's Court-packing plan. But in his "as-told-to" autobiography published in 1962, *Yankee from the West,* the Montanan maintained that he had acted consistently. He had fought the local "big interests" in his home town of Butte during the First World War, he had fought other "big interests" on the national scene in the Twenties, and he had defended the independence of the judiciary against the biggest interest of all, Big Government.

Wheeler and Borah were of course Western insurgents, a fact which has implications that will be followed further in our final chapter. But we must bear in mind also that the Easterner Al Smith had a streak of the states'-righter in him; indeed, since the Democratic Party regularly invoked "Jeffersonianism," with its inescapable animus against concentration, in attacks upon the Republican regimes of the Twenties, the kind of criticism Arthur Schlesinger, Jr., makes on behalf of the Opposition in *The Crisis of the Old Order* may not always be the kind that Opposition would have made if left to its own devices. No less a "progressive" than Franklin Delano Roosevelt went on record during the Twenties as preferring Jefferson over Hamilton—an embarrassment historians of a later day who admire both Hamilton and FDR have never satisfactorily resolved.

If historians have difficulty in resolving questions like these, history itself does resolve them, one way or another. Forces were at work in the Twenties against the continuing littleness of government, forces which carried along both the

Coolidge Administration and its opponents in spite of themselves. In *William Howard Taft: Chief Justice,* Alpheus T. Mason has shown that this holds true even for so conspicuous a stand-patter as his three-hundred-pound hero. As Chief Justice of the United States, ex-President Taft tirelessly pushed administrative reform of the Supreme Court through a recalcitrant Congress, and "the irony of his career," concludes Mason, "is that the revisions he sponsored and pushed through to enactment should now be helpful to causes he profoundly distrusted." But the irony is still deeper, for Taft's judicial opinions themselves, Stanley I. Kutler argues, "ultimately—and decisively—helped weigh the balance toward national power and supremacy," any personal reactionary political convictions to the contrary notwithstanding.

Or consider the curious fate of one "temporary" wartime government agency. The War Finance Corporation, instead of winding up its affairs with the coming of peace, played an unexpected and useful role as a source of loans for agricultural relief in 1921, and in fact the momentum of its establishment carried the agency down to 1929. Then, as Gerald D. Nash has shown, the WFC's managing director, Eugene Meyer, succeeded in effect in re-establishing the institution under a new name, with the same functions and many of the same personnel that the wartime lending agency had had. As the Reconstruction Finance Corporation it would be a major engine of recovery under the New Deal.

Again, Donald C. Swain in a careful study of federal conservation policy from 1921 to 1933 has demonstrated that "contrary to widely held opinion, the national conservation program did not deteriorate in the 1920's. It expanded and matured," even "against the wishes of the Republican chief executives." In the absence of a dramatic leader like Theodore Roosevelt, the conservation movement had to be "sparked by a vigorous bureaucratic leadership," by which Swain seems to imply that once a federal bureau has reached a certain degree of maturity, prestige, and accepted usefulness it can persist and expand and even innovate in the face of widespread apathy and opposition. Richard Kirkendall and others have shown that the same generalization holds for the Department of Agriculture during the Twenties, and indeed President Hoover's own research committee on *Recent Social Trends* was destined to close out his administration with the conclusion that "the further development of American government" faced the nation as "a major and unavoidable problem of modern social life."

If government expansion continued in the face of an ideology of retrenchment, so foreign entanglement continued in the face of an ideology of isolation. In fact William Appleman Williams, in an essay entitled "The Legend of Isolationism in the 1920's," went so far as to brand the latter ideology a myth: "Far from isolation, the foreign relations of the United States from 1920 through 1932 were marked by express and extended involvement with—and intervention in the affairs of—other nations of the world." (The cautious reader should not be put off by the fact that this judgment appeared in the Marxist pages of *Science and Society;* one takes one's scholarship where one finds it.) Not all students of the history of American foreign policy will accept the implications of plan and volition in the statement just quoted, but at the very least one may say that the persons officially concerned with this country's interests abroad could and did manifest the same bureaucratic entrepreneurship that Swain's conservationists displayed at home. This could be true even though they carried on some of their activities in settings as Coolidgean as the "quaint old place" George F. Kennan recalls the State Department had been in the Twenties when he entered it, "with its law-office atmosphere, its cool dark corridors . . . its brass cuspidors, its black leather rocking chairs, and the grandfather's clock in the Secretary of State's office."

In *Prelude to Pearl Harbor: The United States Navy and the Far East, 1921–1931,* Gerald E. Wheeler has recorded an especially striking example of how much could go on even in such cozy environs. It was a time of massive cuts in the federal budget, and the Navy was expensive; it was a time of worldwide naval disarmament, a trend American leaders actively supported, and the Navy was battleship-minded; it was a time when Calvin Coolidge could lightly discuss with his press corps a proposal to turn the Philippines over to the Japanese as a relief measure after the great Tokyo earthquake of 1923, and the Navy was both respectful and suspicious of Japan. Throughout the decade the Navy Department assumed that that Empire's goal was commercial and eventually political hegemony over the Far East, and that if the United States adhered to its own stated commitments in the area the two countries were headed toward collision. Consequently, the American admirals reorganized the fleet, moving most of it for the first time into the Pacific; cadged as much as they could from Congress for modernization, slyly appealing to certain historic prejudices in that body by intimating that the money was needed for defense against the British; and maneuvered and planned against the day they thought was inevitably coming—planned not in terms of coast defense but of a forward encounter with the Japanese Imperial Fleet.

Publicly, the Navy faced the opposition of skeptics like Senator Thomas J. Walsh, who declared in 1928 that "a war with Japan is about as likely as a war with Mars," but some civilians shared the admirals' apprehensions. In 1929 the Hearst reporter Floyd Gibbons wrote a science-fiction melodrama, *The Red Napoleon,* in which he prophesied the deaths of Al Jolson, Florenz Ziegfeld, Colonel Theodore Roosevelt, Jr., and his fellow newsmen Heywood Broun and Arthur "Bugs" Baer in a bombardment of New York City by Asian invaders in 1935, while President Al Smith sent a Christmas Day message from the refugee capital in St. Louis to hard-pressed American forces dug into the ruins of Manhattan, and the aged George M. Cohan sang "Give My Regards to Broadway" over the radio to cheer them on. Gibbons's predicted enemy was a worldwide coalition under a Soviet Genghis Khan, rather than Japan alone, but the *dénouement* of this yarn must have delighted any Navy buff who read it: the defeat of the combined Communist British, French, Italian, Japanese, and German fleets in a kind of super-Jutland just outside the Gulf of Mexico. (A ten-page appendix gave a complete table of organization for both fleets, with the names of all the principal ships!)

It is not likely that Calvin Coolidge would have diverted his mind from the cares of state by reading such tales, as two more recent American Presidents notoriously have, but he does seem to have read some of the Navy's own distress signals. After the failure of the naval limitation conference in Geneva in 1927, Coolidge admitted to the reporters that the economies in naval armament which he had hoped for would now not be possible, and later that year in his annual message to Congress he gave his blessing to "a considerable building program" for the Navy. But the building program did not actually materialize until the Thirties, and one reason may have been that many people found it easy to equate the Navy Department's sober strategic concern with the Hearst newspaperman's sensationalism. If isolationism in the Twenties was a "myth," as William Appleman Williams would have it, it was a myth in which many devoutly believed.

Conceding the "express and extended involvement" of which Williams wrote, in a footnote to his *America's Rise to World Power* (1954), Foster Rhea Dulles at once went on to assert that "American policy during these years remained basically isolationist." Typically, Arthur H. Vandenburg, a Grand Rapids editor whose style already had something of the senatorial flavor of his later years, declared categorically in 1926 that "the prime motive" for "the recent rejection of the League of Nations was the incalculable obligation of a subtle Covenant which bound us, like soldiers of fortune, into all the wars of all the world—a perpetual recruit to Mars." For every American Legion post urging readiness for any eventuality there could be found in the Twenties a church group vowing that America must never again go to war—and as often as not phrasing its concern for peace in terms of isolation from Europe, the place where wars were made.

"We are opposed to any official participation in purely European affairs"; so wrote Franklin Roosevelt in July of 1928, and such also was the philosophy of the Republican administration he and Al Smith were then seeking to oust. Unofficial participation, particularly in European fiscal affairs, was of course extensive and important; from a study such as Joseph Brandes, *Herbert Hoover and Economic Diplomacy,* emerges an impression, perhaps not entirely intended by the author, of Secretary Hoover's tenure in the Commerce Department as representing a major expansion of government functions both foreign and domestic, and ironically enough in business's own name. But Herbert Feis in *The Diplomacy of the Dollar,* a monograph combining brevity with wit, pointed out the inescapable limitations inherent in such an approach: the dollar, in the relative absence of other means to a vigorous assertion either of national influence or of international concord, could not do the job by itself.

Alexander De Conde has proposed a useful distinction between "isolation," as an American doctrine based essentially on the geopolitical facts of life in the nineteenth century, and "isolation*ism*," as the attempt to maintain that doctrine (or rather, "ad hoc strategies and policies" advocated in that doctrine's name) in the face of a twentieth-century reality to which most of those facts had ceased to apply. The twentieth-century isolationists, writes De Conde, "modified some of their ideas to fit the new circumstances but they came out with nineteenth-century conclusions." And Feis's example of a State Department more concerned to prevent the sale of Pilsner Brewery bonds in the United States (as being inconsistent with our Prohibition law) than to prevent the rearmament of a nationalist Germany suggests that the feeling of "isolation," in its original meaning of remoteness from Europe, had extraordinary psychological persistence.

In *Felix Frankfurter Reminisces* (1960), the jurist recalled having chaired a meeting in Boston during the Twenties at which Harold Laski, fresh from a recent encounter with statesmen such as Gandhi and Nehru, lectured brilliantly on the problem of British India; afterward, when the floor was opened for discussion, the second question asked was "What does Professor Laski think of Calvin Coolidge?" And as Frankfurter vainly appealed to the audience, "Do please ask questions pertaining to India," the questioners continued to pepper the English visitor with irrelevancies: what did he think of minimum-wage laws, popular election of judges, unicameralism? America First, in the Twenties, seems to have been as much an inertia as an ideology.

Thus at the psychic level at least, in foreign affairs as in matters domestic, the conventional view of American political life in the Twenties seems to hold up: Babylon was on wheels and nobody was in the driver's seat, even though there were signs that the road ahead might be rough. Ordinarily the subsequent history of the United States Government has been seen by (usually liberal) historians as a series of attempts to grasp hold of the steering wheel, so to speak, either indirectly through the business community (Hoover, Eisenhower) or directly by the power of government (FDR, Kennedy). But the successive frustrations of Presidents—the inability of either Hoover or Roosevelt to reduce unemployment to manageable proportions until an extraneous factor, war, came to the rescue; the inability of Truman to bring into existence a "Fair Deal" program against the refractory will of the Congress; or the inability of Eisenhower to end the Cold War by personal diplomacy at the Summit—suggest that even the most "modern" or "strong" of executives, with the charm of a Roosevelt, the crisp decisiveness of a Truman, or the flair and form of a Kennedy, have had to play to an uncomfortably great extent the role of a Coolidge at times, occupying the seat of highest power at the price of surrendering that power's full exercise.

How could it have been otherwise? In those countries where power *was* unambiguously grasped and exercised, the outcome was terror, as under Stalin, or disaster, as in Japan, or madness, as with the Nazis. To escape a like fate, the democracies' governments had to maintain control that was something less than total: they muddled, as in England, or they improvised, as in North America (the careers of Roosevelt and W. L. Mackenzie King, so different in personal political styles, make an instructive parallel here). In the payoff of the Second World War, it was these bumbling regimes and peoples that turned out to have the qualities necessary to see it through; in that light it may be well to remember that when a contrast with Calvin Coolidge is sought, for executive energy, far-reaching purpose, and the promotion of government action throughout society, the model most readily available in the Twenties was Benito Mussolini.

Indeed, one of the paradoxes of the Twenties is that under a regime as free-running as that of Calvin Coolidge so many should have complained of regimentation and conformity. The complaint itself might be dismissed as a chronic one in any age of the republic's history, especially among intellectuals; as early as 1836, Gulian Verplanck had noted a tendency of the American scholar to dwell upon his society's shortcomings "with a sort of complacent disgust"—except that the Klan atrocities and the library censorship and the labor-baiting of the period were so conspicuously effective. If Big Government could scarcely be blamed for these oppressions, Big Business might have seemed a likely candidate for the villain's role; it was frequently so singled out, and there was certainly enough evidence on the record of the Twenties, of towns dominated, union organizers beaten, and teachers dismissed, to give this charge some substance. "While a good deal of business propaganda and a good many of the activities of strictly business associations . . . had the objective . . . of enlarging the markets for goods, services, and securities," wrote Thomas C. Cochran and William Miller in what remains one of the best among histories of American industrial society, *The Age of Enterprise* (1942), "businessmen also were seeking in every possible way to direct American thinking in lines more favorable to general business purposes. . . . And on the whole, of course, they succeeded."

But the application, in our first chapter, of Leo Lowenthal's hypothesis to the Twenties suggests that whether the businessmen of the Twenties were the movers and shapers of society the businessmen of the Eighties had individually been is open to serious question. At least one outsider who broke into their charmed circle, beat them at their own game, and got safely out again before the stock market carried some of them down was not notably impressed by their power and prestige (though he may later on have changed his mind): "Big businessmen are the most overrated men in the country," Joseph P. Kennedy would one day tell his sons. "Here I am, a boy from East Boston, and I took 'em."

Furthermore, it is not clear by any means that the powers such men did possess were invariably exercised in the direction of concentration and conformity. Apologists for the Gargantuan automotive industry, for one example, have argued that it has generated as many new little businesses as big ones, and may even have "served to 'de-oligopolize' other sectors of the economy that were once considered lost to monopoly." As for social and personal freedom, John Chamberlain maintains, the automobile "has actually worked in a profound sense to save America for the little man. . . . The sixty million cars that are now [1963] traveling the American roads mean that no one is chained to any single way of life"—though urban philosophers like Lewis Mumford, as those same millions of automobiles pour into and choke the cities, might retort that the real problem of reconciling freedom with order begins not on the open road but at the exit ramp.

In any case, in the limitations on liberty of which Americans in the Twenties complained, factors other than private enterprise were surely involved. John Dos Passos, who in those days had no great love for America's business civilization, made the central character in his novel *Manhattan Transfer* cry out, "God I wish I could blame it all on capitalism." Over against both Big Business and Big Government as a force for social conformity and sometimes for individual disintegration stood what might be termed Big Society: "Under the remorseless hammering of the machine was effected a standardization of American society that daily increased in precision and completeness," wrote Charles and Mary Beard. "Nothing escaped its iron strokes. Those who apparently directed and those who labored became one in the routine." Joseph Dorfman notes for example that the Frederick Taylor style of "scientific management," which one ordinarily thinks of as being of the quintessence of American capitalism (and regimentation) during the Twenties, "goes back to a Fourierite idea," and found favor in America among socialists as well as businessmen.

It is important that we not fall into the same mistake that the men of the Twenties made and assume that the American cultural or economic experience was unique and isolated. As well as an American Twenties there were a British, a French, a Weimar German, even a Soviet and a Japanese Twenties, and much of what took place here may have been the expression, or preview, of what is likely to happen in all industrial cultures at a certain stage of development. The impersonal processes of urbanization, machine technology, and mass communication seem inescapable, whether they are nominally presided over by a Calvin Coolidge or a Ramsay MacDonald, a capitalist or a socialist, or for that matter a monarch or a revolutionary committee of generals. (Whether these forces make specifically for *social* conformity is of course a more open question; it is always possible that William Graham Sumner was right, and that even in the Machine Age the more archaic processes he described in *Folkways* remain decisive.)

Whatever the precise causative agent at work, such that the individual felt bullied, or neglected, or altogether lost in modern society, one obvious way of transcending the shortcomings of any social order is available in any historical age. From the silent intimacy of the Friends' Meeting to the soaring spaces of the cathedral, the many modes of traditional religion proclaim man's ultimate worth. Even within a social organization as enormous as the Roman Catholic Church there is room for the prayers and concerns of an individual lighting a votive candle— but the Twenties were not a particularly auspicious time to apply that kind of remedy to the patient. A YMCA survey of the religious beliefs prevalent in the American Expeditionary Force in France, published in 1920, disclosed a vagueness in the content of what was believed coupled with acrid criticism of its institutional forms; the editors concluded that if the Army draftees surveyed were a representative cross-section of the people then "America is not a Christian nation in any strictly religious sense."

Such continued to be the tenor of sociological inquiry. Robert and Helen Lynd, in the chapter on "Religious Observances" in their classic study of *Middletown,* found that "religious life as represented by the churches is less pervasive than a generation ago," and in 1933 Hornell Hart, summarizing the topics discussed in magazines indexed in the *Reader's Guide* for his chapter in the massive cooperative study *Recent Social Trends,* concluded that "religious sanctions have been largely displaced by scientific sanctions in discussions published in leading magazines," and furthermore that "antagonistic criticism of the church, of ministers and of traditional creeds reached a maximum in 1925–1928 in general magazines, and still exceeds the volume of favorable comment." Statistics of formal allegiance to churches seemed to bear this out; in another of the chapters in the same

study, C. Luther Fry conceded that "in the last twenty years
. . . religious bodies have made far more impressive gains in
wealth than in membership," the Roman Catholic Church included. And the federal government's census of religious bodies
for the decade 1926–1936 disclosed that for the first time in
American history the "mainstream" WASP denominations in
the North—for example, Methodists, Congregationalists, Pres-
byterians—showed an actual net membership decline.

To be sure the decline was not irreversible. After the Second
World War, all of the churches, for reasons about which intellectuals in and out of church are still arguing, began to grow
even faster than the population, and seemingly to take an
upsurge in prestige and felt relevance also. But this development
could scarcely have been foreseen in the Twenties; on the basis
of the evidence available to them the forecasters of *Recent Social
Trends* were justified in stating that "extrapolation of trends
suggests the probable further decline of interest and belief in
traditional Christianity, as herein defined." Meditating upon
this cycle of decline and revival, Robert T. Handy for his presidential address to the American Society of Church History in
1959 chose the title "The American Religious Depression,
1925–1935"; for Protestantism, at least—apart from the Fundamentalist wing, which will be considered in more detail in our
final chapter—the phrase seems both apt and just.

Because of the "long-standing identification of Protestantism with American culture," Handy argued, that branch of organized religion in America was "left . . . quite exposed to
cultural cross-currents," and was therefore peculiarly vulnerable
when those currents set in a direction unfavorable to religion in
general. In another work the present writer has attempted to
identify some of those currents: the persuasive power of popular
science (what Handy calls "scientism, behaviorism, and hu-
manism"); the eloquent anticlerical polemics of men like
Mencken and Clarence Darrow; the rising generation's aver-
sion to Prohibition, Victorian moralism, and philistinism, with

all of which the churches were associated; the widespread dis-
illusionment over the First World War, in which the churches
had played a shabby propagandizing role; and their equally
shabby identification with the business ethic at its most business-
like and least ethical, of which Bruce Barton's admiring
biography of Christ the Go-Getter was only the most flagrant
example. When the religious depression had run its course,
this combination of forces would no longer be fully operative,
but the "successful" churches of the Sixties would be open to
the same basic criticism as the "unsuccessful" churches of the
Twenties: they could not redeem the individual from the inhumanity of mass society because they themselves had taken on
many of the lineaments of that society.

Already in the Twenties the theologically more liberal
churches in particular manifested a drive for keeping up with
the Joneses at all costs. In the Lynds' *Middletown,* "spiritual"
values seem to have modulated into a kind of *civisme* ("The
baffling too-bigness of European wars, death, . . . ill health,
business worries, and political graft . . . all shrinks at a
championship basket-ball game or a Chamber of Commerce
rally, and the whole business of living in Middletown suddenly
'fits' again . . . ."), even while religious joy was being displaced in the churches themselves by a brisk and cheery good
fellowship more akin to that of the Elks and Kiwanis. A re-
tired minister recalls an assistant pastorate in a church at a
busy intersection in Providence, Rhode Island, toward the end
of the Twenties: "There were Scout troops, community boys'
athletics, church school athletics, social service clubs, mothers'
clubs—almost every activity imaginable, and incidentally a
church."

In such a church, whose pastor might refer to it quite
unself-consciously as "our plant," the tone of worship itself
was bound to change. In a city church filled on a Sunday morn-
ing with an "audience" rather than a "congregation," Herbert
Schneider has observed, "the service is more of a professional

performance, less a community expression or folk art" than it had been when the parish was founded on a geographic neighborhood. At its worst, the service strained to be novel and up-to-date in the same pathetic way some adults try to keep up with the nuances of teen slang, and ultimately with as little success. The traditional hymn-sing was rebilled on the church bulletin board as a "Snappy Song Service"; the offertory might be enlivened by having an usher blow a whistle whenever someone dropped a dollar bill in the plate (one such ministerial entrepreneur's "temple reverberated with 105 toots on that particular Sabbath," Robert Moats Miller reports); and the sermon's text was likely to be taken from the latest edition of the newspaper and its titles from the slogans of mass-media advertising. There was small comfort in such a Consumers' Church for the refugee from the consumers' world.

So far these comments have applied chiefly to Protestantism. Professor Handy, following the federal census returns, noted that "Jewish congregations enjoyed a healthy growth in the 1926–36 decade," and that by 1941 the Catholic Church in America had come out of the "religious depression" with such strength as to prompt one Catholic-convert historian, Theodore Maynard, to declare: "Except for isolated 'fundamentalists' . . . Catholicism could cut through Protestantism as through so much butter." But, Handy adds, "Neither Judaism nor Catholicism was embarrassed by too close identification with the surrounding culture"—a bit of an understatement, considering the Klan parades and gentlemen's agreements and restriction of immigration that marked the postwar decade. Under fire in the Twenties from super-patriotic groups for alleged un-Americanism, the Catholic hierarchy "shelved" the ambitious Bishops' Program for social action which had been formulated during the First World War, "lest it be used against Catholic interests," Aaron Abell has written. As for Judaism, it has seemed to Nathan Glazer that that faith in twentieth-century America "is even more vulnerable to the unsettling influence of modernity than is Christianity."

The politically conscious churchman, struggling to apply his religion directly to the criticism and reformation of Big Society, was in a particularly desperate plight. After six chapters on the vicissitudes of liberalism in the Protestant churches during the Twenties, the present writer concluded in 1956 that "the Social Gospel as it stood in 1920 and the decade thereafter was living on borrowed time." Robert Moats Miller has dissented in part, and urged historians to use "slightly less somber hues" to depict social Christianity in the Twenties; but Donald B. Meyer, in his thoughtful, somewhat Tillichian study of religion and politics in that period continued to paint in chiaroscuro: "Protestantism was entering a period of complexity and defeat" at the beginning of the Twenties, an era in which the social-gospel vanguard would find themselves increasingly isolated both from the culture and from their fellow churchmen.

In Judaism, judging from a perceptive study by Leonard J. Mervis of "The Social Justice Movement and the American Reform Rabbi," this isolation seems to have been felt less acutely, for, whereas "individuals of other denominations have turned to social religion," Reform Judaism had committed "its total self" to the religious quest for social justice. (Whether Mervis meant the entire membership, or the Reform clergy only, in this assertion is not clear; probably the latter—which makes a world of difference in interpretation.) But the Catholic liberal in the Twenties, "an age of retreat when holding actions, limited counter-offensives, and prayer were the only recourse," as Francis L. Broderick puts it, was in a peculiarly awkward situation.

In *Right Reverend New Dealer,* Broderick depicts the dilemma of one such liberal, Monsignor John A. Ryan. Estranged from such Catholic prelates as William Cardinal O'Connell, who threw the formidable weight of the Boston arch-

E

diocese into the 1924 state election to defeat the ratification by Massachusetts of a proposed federal child labor amendment, a man like Father Ryan was often estranged also from secular liberals over issues in which his, and the Church's, stand differed from theirs. (The exchange of letters between Ryan and Norman Thomas over the Mexican crisis of 1927, published in the *Catholic Historical Review* in 1959, is an especially poignant example.) "A friend of liberal reformers, Protestant leaders, and American Catholics," Broderick summarizes, "Ryan ran the danger that each group might embarrass him with the others." All that it seemed possible for such a person to do in the Twenties to resolve such a dilemma was to wait for the historical situation to change, frustrating counsel indeed for a man of action.

But perhaps activism was out of place for reform-minded persons, religious or otherwise. Programmatic solutions of any kind to the problems of modernity may have been premature in the Twenties. Clarke Chambers cites a 1929 judgment on the "shaky premises" of the older Progressivism by one veteran social-actionist, Donald Richberg: "What was right and what was wrong more frequently required the test of scientific analysis than of popular opinion." In short, it was necessary to know before one could act. Such seems to have been the view of James Harvey Robinson in 1921 when he declared "I have no reforms to recommend except the liberation of intelligence."

Commenting upon that statement a quarter-century afterward, Morton White found Robinson's recommendation as vague as anything proposed by President Harding. But before the still younger reader, conditioned by the actionist Sixties, concurs too quickly in White's criticism he should remember that men like Robinson supposed that the liberation of intelligence was a real possibility. To respond to the cruelties and absurdities of one's society by writing a book on *Mind in the Making* might have been an evasion, but it was also an act of faith, in which Robinson was joined by a small army of publicists and popularizers who conscientiously wrote to instruct, entertain, and (hopefully) liberate the mind of the "general reader" or "man in the street."

It was and is easy to fault such writers and their readers, as Frederick Hoffman seems to, for having sought only "a plausible substitute for the simplicity of the Sunday sermon," in the popular-science field especially. But James Steele Smith, in an essay "The Day of the Popularizers: The 1920's," replies that even the most simplistic of these interpreters of human knowledge had "a happy energy . . . in striking contrast to the sober, sometimes wry weariness of many contemporary 'general writers' on science and culture, loaded down by their sense of the loneliness of intellect and the mental emptiness of crowds." This American trend is closely related to a similar British concern for popular instruction, typified in the Victorian age by Thomas Huxley's lectures on evolution before working-class audiences and in the Twenties by the popular-science writings of his grandson Julian in collaboration with H. G. Wells, as well as the popular history Wells wrote on his own. W. Warren Wagar, in *H. G. Wells and the World State,* has argued that both Wells and his American equivalents (such as Robinson), usually dismissed as pamphleteers, ought to be taken seriously as a chapter in intellectual history; and indeed in both Britain and the United States many a young reader grown older can still acknowledge an early debt to *The Outline of History* or *Why We Behave Like Human Beings* or even, Smith and Wagar might have added, *The Stars for Sam.*

The makers of popular books were not the only persons following James Harvey Robinson's recommendation. In *The Transformation of the School,* Lawrence A. Cremin has described the institutionalization during the Twenties of progressive education, which had also been conceived originally as a means to the liberation of intelligence. But shorn of most of its radical, social-reconstructionist animus by the community pressures of the time—and by the introduction of principles of "scientific management" and other concepts borrowed from business (a process documented by Raymond E. Callahan in *Education and the Cult of Efficiency*)—the progressive education movement turned from socially-oriented goals to expressionist and Freudian concerns for self-fulfillment; Cremin cites one educational experimenter of the Twenties who explicitly rejected social change in favor of individual regeneration, for all the world like an old-fashioned evangelical revivalist: "One could do nothing with social groups as they then existed," reasoned Margaret Naumburg in 1928, "but one could do something with individuals, who would later reform the groups they joined." The school's rejoinder to Big Society, then, was not one of preachment or social action; rather, declared the authors of *The Child-Centered School* (also published in 1928), "the task of the school is to surround the child with an environment which will draw out [his] creative power." "Once the creative power had been released in a generation of American children," comments Cremin, "the authors held little fear of the future."

On the other hand, Cremin is historically aware that "the doctrine of creative self-expression raised the same problems in education as it raised elsewhere," and he sadly concedes that "in too many classrooms license began to pass for liberty, planlessness for spontaneity, recalcitrance for individuality, obfuscation for art, and chaos for education." Stow Persons is still more harsh: in twentieth-century America, he wrote in 1958, "it became increasingly evident that the schools and even the colleges were places where children, instead of growing up, retained the privilege of remaining children."

Richard Hofstadter, in the three trenchant chapters on education in his *Anti-intellectualism in American Life,* has raised a still more disturbing possibility: that progressive education in its ultimate avatar as "life-adjustment" would become neither a laboratory for social experiment nor a means to individual expression, but a vehicle for domesticating children into Big Society: "to help them learn the ways of the world of consumption and hobbies" rather than "to fit them to become a disciplined part of the world of production and competition, ambition and vocation"—all of which would have astonished John Dewey, but comes to the reader of Leo Lowenthal's essay on mass idols as the fulfillment of a prophecy.

Yet the post-Sputnik reaction against "life-adjustment" education has produced some equally unpleasant consequences, in the tense, highly competitive, anxiety-ridden, and joyless round of existence which can be observed at all educational levels, from the nightmare of getting into a good kindergarten to the senior professor's nagging doubt that he really is a productive scholar after all. Said one moppet to another boarding a school bus, in the popular caricaturist Lichty's syndicated "Grin and Bear It" cartoon one day late in 1966, "Look at it this way, Otis—school is just a mouse race to prepare us for the rat race."

But "we weren't that way" in school, declared William C. Devane, Yale '20, in a 1965 interview. "We had time for fun." As was noted in our first chapter, any reminiscence is suspect; still, Professor Devane, who had been Dean of Yale College for twenty-five of the intervening years, made out a strong case. "What the students had in those days," as the Associated Press summarized Devane's remarks, "was an air of lightheartedness, gaiety, privacy, leisure. . . . There was time for classmate Thornton Wilder to begin his playwriting and Stephen Vincent Benét his books"—and not as projects for academic credit, he might have added. F. Scott Fitzgerald after all was a Princeton "dropout," but with an entirely different set of connotations from those which the word carries today.

The adverse critic of the Twenties might reply that the modern student, unlike his Jazz Age counterpart, has discovered that Life is real, Life is earnest—were it not for the fact that the private, leisured, and even "bohemian" side of life in the Twenties could itself be pursued with a kind of moral earnestness. Not always; Helen Lynd has commented tellingly

on the "code of the pose" in the 1920's, by which one protected oneself from being made ridiculous by invoking the all-
purpose adjective "amusing." But in his exasperating though
provocative book *Yankees and God,* Chard Powers Smith cate-
gorized the seventeenth century in America as the World of the
Cosmos, the eighteenth century as the World of Man, the early
nineteenth century as the World of Men, and the Twenties as
the World of Me—all four of which, he maintained, were varia-
tions on the single theme of Puritanism!

At times indeed the pathway of the seeker after self-fulfillment in the Twenties seems to have been as bestrewn with
moral do's and don't's as the way of any seventeenth-century
pilgrim. Don't be old-fashioned, don't be hypocritical, don't
be a prude; and, do be brave, do obey the unconscious (D. H.
Lawrence's "dark gods"), and do be honest with your own
mind and emotions. It is the paradox later to be described by
Sartre, of man as "condemned to be free." If man is totally free
to act, then he is totally responsible for what he chooses (elects,
in the theological sense of the word) and creates, in the place
of God—surely a burden more terrifying than any the erstwhile
Puritans had laid down; and at the same time, it is the most
radical possible rejection of the claims of Big Society.

But are we warranted in reading a philosophical vogue that
followed the Second World War back into the situation which
followed the First? John Killinger has made out a case that we
are, for at least one key figure of the Twenties, in *Hemingway
and the Dead Gods.* Properly noting that "there has been
no known liaison between him and the existentialists," apart
from however much of that philosophic spirit Hemingway may
have imbibed in the same Paris bars and cafes that Sartre and
his friends were later to frequent, Killinger portrays the novelist
as having been in effect an existentialist without the vocabulary.

"When you go to war as a boy," Hemingway was to write
during a later war, "you have a great illusion of immortality.
Other people get killed; not you. . . . Then when you are

badly wounded the first time you lose that illusion." Once the illusion is lost—in Sartrian terms, once one accepts fully the fact that authentic Being is always in the shadow of Nothingness (*nada,* in Hemingway's vocabulary)—then, and then only, can one become free, knowing in Hemingway's case that "Whatever I had to do men had always done"; and what one does *is,* by that definition, one's morality. Morality is not "given," by the culture, by the propagandists, by the Others; "glory," "honor," "hallow" for Hemingway become obscenities when they are thus applied to the awful reality of a modern battlefield. These words are made real only moment by moment in the choices and chances of the fight, and they may legitimately be remembered only as "the numbers of roads, the names of rivers, the names of regiments and the dates." "This," Killinger comments, "is existential sentiment, emphasizing the very real kinship between the philosophy of existence and the science of phenomenology: value is only in living, not in abstractions."

As a personal adaptation for emotional survival, learned in a situation of routinized mass-slaughter and applied afterward in a situation of routinized dehumanization, this mutation of romantic hero into tough-hearted stoic has commended itself to many. Speaking for "young men born between 1918, roughly, and 1924," John W. Aldridge confessed that Hemingway's "impact upon us was tremendous. . . . We could follow him, ape his manner . . . through all the doubts and fears of adolescence and come out pure and untouched." The Hemingway style has seemed to some a viable answer to the moral problem posed by standardized mass-consumption, mindless organization, and the discipline of the time-clock. Without attempting to recover the irrevocable past, Hemingway seems to say that "in our time" the demeaning and dehumanizing forces of Big Society can be transcended by the grace of primary experience met with courage and good form.

But as an *ideology*—and if Aldridge and his contemporaries really did take Hemingway's words as conveying experience so exactly "that we began unconsciously to translate our own sensations into their terms and to impose on everything we did and felt the particular emotions they aroused in us," then it is indeed possible to speak of "Hemingwayism" in ideological terms—this tough-guy philosophy is nevertheless vulnerable. Lewis Mumford has condemned in particular the rise of a "morality of the 'dead pan' " which treats "normal emotions as deplorably sentimental and strong emotions as simply hysterical or funny"—a morality which, although Mumford does not say so, probably owes something to a simplified version of the Hemingwayist ideology. And that Hemingway "code," for example (of which Killinger's analysis makes a great deal), sometimes proliferates into such minutiae that it borders on the ludicrous; not only must the kill be well and cleanly done, but on the fishing trip in *Big Two-Hearted River* the coffee in the can must be well and truly boiled, and the reader begins to feel like an intruder at a Boy Scout jamboree.

Antibourgeois though the Hemingway code was intended to be, it was anticlimactically middle-class American in one important assumption, namely that hardship and violence are something one has to go out and look for. Jonathan Daniels has ironically noted that Oak Park, Illinois, the home town from which the novelist went out to hunt and fight, also sent Bruce Barton out into the rather less lethal world of Madison Avenue. He might have added that some of Hemingway's other contemporaries, such as the Negro writers of the "Harlem Renaissance" of the Twenties (Countee Cullen, Langston Hughes, Claude McKay), did not have to attend bullfights or go on safaris or enlist in wars in order to have experiences rugged enough to draw upon for their art!

Leslie A. Fiedler reminds us that the Hemingway hero, who "returns again and again to the fishing trip and the journey to the war—those two traditional evasions of domesticity and civil life," is not a new creation of the Twenties but is in fact an archetype; that fictional American men perennially have recoiled from home, marriage, and maturity by shipping out for two years before the mast or descending into maelstroms or fighting the Indians in the West or harpooning whales with Queequeg. If there is truth in this vision of the American past, then the Hemingway hero or disciple in real life faces in the midtwentieth century a doom ironically different from the messy but dignified death the Master envisioned. "Natty Bumppo gives way to the bounty-hunter, to Buffalo Bill," Fiedler writes, "and Buffalo Bill is followed by the dude with pack animal and guide and whisky bottle, playing Indian and fleeing his wife." To put it into Leo Lowenthal's categories— or Veblen's—Big Society increasingly transforms all primary experience into goods that it vends at second hand for consumption (the mountain is closed except to licensed climbers, the suburbs swarm out over the game preserves, the prize-fight becomes vaudeville), and the dream of self-realization through the simple life of adventure and inarticulate comradeship becomes a mocking will-o'-the-wisp.

How compelling, and at the same time how ultimately quixotic, such a dream could become in the Twenties has been explored in an essay by John William Ward. The solo crossing of the Atlantic in 1927 by Charles A. Lindbergh seems to have furnished something of a moral catharsis for that generation of Americans; indeed, Ward concluded, "The grubbiness of the twenties had a good deal to do with the shining quality of Lindbergh's success." "The world understood," Walter Lippmann wrote admiringly in 1929, "that here was somebody who was altogether braver than the average sensual man" or, to put it into Hemingway-ese, Lindbergh had well and truly flown. And something of the spell of the *Spirit of St. Louis* could still evoke a response in the Sixties: "He flew alone. And on a single engine," said a *Time* Essay on the fortieth anniversary of Lindbergh's flight. "He was the first real hero of the machine age, and in a sense the last."

In that concluding phrase the *Time* essayist followed the reasoning of Professor Ward, who marked the extraordinary choice of title for the young flier's first book—it was *We,* himself and the airplane—and asked: "Was the flight the achievement of a heroic, solitary, unaided individual? Or did the flight represent the triumph of the machine, the success of an industrially organized society?" Americans in the Twenties, Ward concluded, were trying to have it both ways, celebrating a pioneer tradition of individualism and at the same time the coming discipline of machine technology, a polarity Arnold Toynbee might forebodingly have called an instance of Archaism-and-Futurism.

In 1964, Lindbergh himself added an elegiac note to this discussion. As he watched the airline stewardesses bustling with their trays thirty-five thousand feet above "the same cold-water ocean I crossed in 1927," the former Lone Eagle confessed that the taming of the air into triviality by countless scheduled crossings had "dull[ed] the sense of magic I felt then in using wings. Now it is progress that impresses me in flying, rather than adventure." And yet he was not altogether convinced. Lying under an acacia tree a few days later in Kenya in the early dawn, the flier meditated upon the simplicity of airplane construction as compared with the evolution of birds, and mused that if he had to choose he "would rather have birds than airplanes." Meeting some painted and spear-wielding Masai warriors, Lindbergh reflected that the replacement of poisoned arrows by atomic bombs was not a convincing argument for the advancement of civilization. The irony is double: a man who had once been decorated by a German government which had had in mind altogether different plans for Africa now was ready in all sincerity to doubt that his own "framework of life" was basically superior to that of the Masai; and this confession of mistrust in Big Society appeared in the pages of one of the most massive of Big Society's media, the *Reader's Digest.*

"Is Civilization Progress?" the aviator asked. No doubt

a high proportion of Lindbergh's contemporaries, in the Sixties or in the Twenties, would have answered with a resounding "yes." For every Hemingway fleeing from the complexity of Big Society and in the process stripping the language to a deceptively "simple" medium for the evocation of nonverbal primary experience there was a John Dos Passos, facing up to the complexities and inventing a rhetoric which would not merely describe but would itself actually resemble the mechanized life that was its subject. "The function of poetry in a Machine Age," Hart Crane bravely declared in 1929, "is identical to its function in any other age," and poetry would fail of its contemporary function unless it could "absorb the machine . . . as naturally and as casually as trees, cattle, galleons, castles and all other human associations of the past." In the bridges and skyscrapers which such a machine technology was bringing forth, the aged Louis Sullivan saw the promise of a vigorous, humane civilization rejoicing in the full use of its powers, material and spiritual; and if Sullivan's younger contemporary Lewis Mumford disapproved of some of the specific results of that technology—"fixed and stereotyped and blank, like the mind of a Robot . . . an architecture fit only for lathes and dynamos to dwell in"—still this criticism was rooted in the modern situation, not some lost Utopia of Greek temples or wattled huts.

Yet even those most determined to come to grips with modernity have had their moments of despair. "The evil institutions that accompanied the rise of the ancient city have been resurrected and magnified in our own time," Mumford would write in 1961; ". . . the emancipation from manual labor has brought about a new kind of enslavement: abject dependence upon the machine." With rueful irony, Matthew Josephson admitted in 1962 that he and those of his associates in the Twenties who "had bravely announced our 'acceptance' of the Machine Age" seemed to have made little impression on Big Society: "We had the effect of a few people firing off peashooters at the unbreakable plate glass-and-steel facade of our civilization." And Hart Crane, Waldo Frank wrote in a new preface to the poems of that would-be bard of the Machine Age, found himself in "a jungle of machines and disintegrating values which he had no discipline or method to manage and which soon destroyed him." Three years after the Crash, Crane stepped off the stern of a New York-bound liner, three hundred miles north of Havana.

As for the singular achievement of John Dos Passos in simulating the blinking-light, random-encounter, film montage quality of Megalopolis in both the form and content of his *Manhattan Transfer,* it is more a dissection than an embrace. Significantly, the most positive and "sympathetic" character in the novel is shown in its closing pages hitch-hiking out of the city, in full flight from Big Society. And Dos Passos's Jimmy Herf, still buoyant as he walked out of New York in 1925, would be mutated into Vag, the hopeless wanderer beside the endless road at the end of *U.S.A.* For a writing generation also busily rejecting the "out-there" world of the farm and small town, Dos Passos's implicit moral was a counsel of desperation: if the kaleidoscope of the city refracted the individual into fragments, and the face-to-face tyranny of the small town strangled him, where was he to go?

The dilemma of a man of the Twenties, trapped between an Old Society which cramped his style and a Big Society which seemed to have no room in it for style at all, was indeed poignant, but its resolution was not to be accomplished by literati, however gifted. "The machine's sudden entrance into the garden," Leo Marx wrote in 1964, "presents a problem that ultimately belongs not to art but to politics"—and if the best that art in America had to offer in the Twenties was the code of Ernest Hemingway, the best that politics had to offer was the code of Calvin Coolidge.

Charles Marion Russell forsook St. Louis for Montana in 1880 when he was only sixteen. . . .

Asked to address a Montana booster meeting shortly before his death in 1926, the old man was horrified to hear himself introduced as a "pioneer." Misty-eyed, he roared: "In my book, a pioneer is a man who comes to a virgin country, traps off all the fur, kills off all the wild meat, cuts down all the trees, grazes off all the grass, plows the roots up, and strings ten million miles of bob wire. A pioneer destroys things and calls it civilization. I wish to God that this country was just like it was when I first saw it, and that none of you folks were here at all!"

ALEXANDER ELIOT, Three Hundred Years
of American Painting (1957)

THREE

Of Town and Country

Much that happened to America in the Twenties has had parallels in other times. The renascent Ku Klux Klan of the Twenties not only evoked memories of Reconstruction but also prefigured the renascent Klan of a day closer to our own. The sexual revolution associated with the Jazz Age brings to mind both the campus philosophers of the Sixties preaching freer love and the presidential candidate of 1884, Grover Cleveland, calmly acknowledging its practice. Many other examples could be found, but from time to time in exploring the Twenties one comes upon something for which there is no exact equivalent in any other period of American history. Such a phenomenon was Prohibition.

In *The Age of Reform,* Richard Hofstadter remarked that the story of the Volstead Act, for "the historian who likes to trace the development of the great economic issues and to follow the main trend of class politics," must seem "a historical detour, a meaningless nuisance, an extraneous imposition upon the main course of history." And yet it will not do to account for an historical phenomenon simply by calling it names. Lawrence W. Levine in his study of the last years of William Jennings Bryan has reminded us that the political battles of the Twenties, of which the one over Prohibition was one of the most bitterly fought, were fully as momentous for the participants as the more broadly-phrased political and economic controversies of the Progressive Era had been for the previous generation. "To call an era marked by conflicts of this nature one of apathy or complacence is inaccurate," Levine writes. "To millions of Americans in the Twenties these"—the struggles over Prohibition, religion, immigration, the rights of minorities—"were the conflicts and issues which were of primary importance, and it was into these channels that they poured their idealism and fervor and energy."

If one temptation of the historian is to shrug Prohibition aside as irrelevant to the major thrust of modern history, another is its opposite: to be captivated by the sheer uniqueness of the phenomenon. Andrew Sinclair titled one study of the movement *Prohibition: The Era of Excess.* But the Thirties, the Forties, and even the flabby Fifties were in their various ways all "eras of excess," and since the publication of Sinclair's book, Ray Ginger has written of the years from 1877 to 1914 in America as an *Age of Excess;* the title as applied to the period of the Eighteenth Amendment is thus not very informative. But a title is not a book; what is more serious is that Sinclair, whose British background might have given him an ironic and detached view of the matter, has chosen retroactively to enlist in the wars of the "Wets" and the "Drys" as a partisan and impassioned Wet.

Were there no more to the Dry crusade than our post-Repeal caricature of it, these polar reactions would be more understandable. But it was not a simple matter of the yokels and the old folks and the reactionaries against the cosmopolites and the young folks and the liberals. At least in the movement's incipient stages, the prohibitionists did not feel that they were fighting the drinker—not, at any rate, the working-class drinker, who was in their view a victim of social injustice, debauched by the same system that robbed him. Rather, they felt they were fighting that system itself, in the spirit of any other Populist or Progressive crusader, as monographs on Prohibition like those of James H. Timberlake, Gilman Ostrander, and Norman H. Clark have made clear.

After Prohibition had become law, there was an inevitable shift in its meaning, but the older humane ideal never quite died out. Upton Sinclair, who has never been classed among the reactionaries, wrote an antiliquor novel which was published only two years before Repeal, and indeed the old socialist returned to the same theme in a work of nonfiction, *The Cup of Fury,* which appeared as late as 1957. For welfare-minded persons in the Twenties, Clarke Chambers has written, "Prohibition was a divisive issue, particularly for professional settlement workers and caseworkers who were increasingly torn between their sure knowledge that alcohol so often meant unhappiness for their neighbors and clients, and their commitment to personal liberty." Of the three-score busy social workers who took time to reply to a letter soliciting the support of welfare workers throughout the nation for Al Smith in 1928, forty-five declared for Hoover (including Jane Addams), seventeen for Smith, two for Norman Thomas—and "many who declared they might otherwise support Smith protested they could not vote against a man who promised the honest and efficient administration of the Eighteenth Amendment."

As a matter of fact, in this controversy the ordinary lines between "liberal" and "conservative" in American politics seem to have become hopelessly snarled. In 1924 a memorable debate took place between the Reverend John Haynes Holmes, a lifelong spokesman for the "social gospel," and Clarence Darrow over the issue of Prohibition. Holmes justified the Volstead Act because, he argued, liquor "creates poverty, it cultivates crime, it . . . constitutes a deliberate exploitation of the weak by the strong." Then Darrow, well known as a defender of the weak against exploitation by the strong, replied in language almost identical to that used by Barry Goldwater to justify his Senate vote against the Civil Rights Act of 1964: the Volstead Act "has made spies and detectives, snooping around doors and windows. It has made informers of thousands of us." And we are reminded with a considerable sense of shock that Prohibition in the Twenties actually was attacked and defended with the same vehemence—including the drumfire accompaniment of violence—with which civil-rights legislation was to be attacked and defended in the Sixties.

Sinclair's book made much of the Southern racist argument for Prohibition, that this restriction was one more way of keeping the Negro in his place. But a Southern racist could also argue *against* Prohibition in terms of the same prejudices. Senator Oscar Underwood of Alabama, more moderate on the race question than most of his colleagues from the South, nevertheless argued in 1928 that the Wet areas of the Northeast were "justified" in making the Eighteenth Amendment virtually inoperative by massive disobedience, in the same way that he thought the areas of the South with a large Negro population and potential electorate were "justified" in making the Fourteenth Amendment practically a dead letter. And in tones reminiscent of those of Richard B. Russell many years later, Underwood invoked traditional Southern political doctrine to condemn Prohibition because it "challenged the integrity of the compact between the States" and compelled men "to live their lives in the mold prescribed by the power of government."

Argument makes strange bedfellows. Walter Lippmann, poles apart from the Alabama senator on questions of civil rights but at one with him on the question of drinking rights, argued in *Harper's* for December, 1926, that the nullification of an undesired law was "a normal and traditional American method of circumventing the inflexibility of the Constitution," and President-Emeritus Hadley of Yale called nullification a "safety valve which helps a self-governing community avoid the alternative between tyranny and revolution." So one visualizes Americans of that period defending violation of the law on the high philosophic grounds of John C. Calhoun—or, to choose a "liberal" metaphor, answering the bootlegger's furtive knock on the kitchen door with a sense of righteousness as assured as if they had been harboring fugitive slaves.

Robert Moats Miller wisely observes: "Nothing is more difficult than for an individual indifferent to a certain issue to appreciate that to others it might be of transcendent importance." But was the right to drink, or the right to be protected from the perils of drinking, really *that* important? If it was, Prohibition cannot be dismissed as an extraneous intrusion on the course of history; and if it was not, then the sense of that importance—what the progressive educators would call its "felt need"—has somehow to be accounted for.

One reason for the felt importance of the liquor issue in the Twenties was that it was one form taken by rural-urban conflict in the same period. The dry areas of the nation roughly coincided with the old Bryan country of the Nineties and the coming Goldwater country of the later Fifties, a point made convincingly by the maps accompanying Andrew Sinclair's book. The urban East's representatives in Congress voted to sustain Woodrow Wilson's veto of the Volstead Act, while those of the rural South and West voted to override it; and the editor of the

F

Anti-Saloon League's *Yearbook,* mindful perhaps of the old adage that the Roman Empire did not so much fall as pass out, warned in 1931 that "great city domination is the rock upon which past civilizations have been wrecked." Judging from what was said about the country and the small town in the fiction of the same period, these sentiments were cordially reciprocated in the city.

But why did the feud between town and country, which after all is universal in human history, take the specific form of Prohibition only once, and in but one major nation of western Christendom? Perhaps the conclusions of Leo Lowenthal's mass-media study are relevant here. If in the Twenties ours was truly becoming a consumer society, such that greater stress is put, figuratively and literally, on what one takes in than on what one puts out; if the linkage between the little man and the great consists essentially in the goods they consume in common (the old "Man Of Distinction" whisky advertisements are a case in point); if indeed consumership is becoming a surrogate for concrete accomplishment, as Veblen had maintained even before the turn of the century, mentioning ceremonial drinking (and drunkenness!) as one of his anthropological examples—then one can better understand how, in the transitional Twenties, the right to drink could have been regarded as being on the same exalted level with the right to vote.

The Lowenthal thesis may also be related to the rural-urban conflict of the Twenties in a more direct way. The older values of the primary producer would have persisted longer in places where they remained necessary for day-to-day survival, such as the family-sized farm; compare the discovery by David Riesman and his associates (in *Faces in the Crowd, The Lonely Crowd*'s less widely read sequel) of their purest example of an "other-directed" personality in a Hollywood press agent and of their most clear-cut specimen of the "inner-directed" type in a Vermont handicraftsman. To be sure the battle-lines between the producers of grain and the consumers of alcohol were disrupted by a high volume of informal trading with the enemy, through the good offices of the Chicago mercantile association headed by "Scarface" Al Capone and a host of lesser industrialists of the hillside still and the city bathtub, but battle-lines they nevertheless were.

Town and country have been putting each other down, with opposing stereotypes of the country bumpkin and the city slicker, at least since the barefoot prophets of ancient Israel left their flocks and herds in the hills to go down and denounce the sophisticated sins of Jerusalem. In more modern times the old feud was given a lease on life by the discovery of the New World; "If European society was in any sense 'urban'," wrote Eric Lampard in the *American Historical Review* (1961), "then the city was part of the bag of tricks rejected in 1776." From Jefferson, who surely was no Anti-Saloon Leaguer, to Bryan, who certainly was, that rejection persisted, and in the Twenties it flowered in three new rural crusades against urban wickedness: Prohibition, Fundamentalism, and the campaign to defeat Al Smith.

Note that the last-mentioned of these crusades is here called "the campaign to defeat Al Smith" rather than "anti-Catholicism." It used to be assumed that these were one and the same thing, until another Catholic candidate began his drive for the Presidency in the late Fifties; and then, as historians and political reporters scented the possibility of a Kennedy victory, they began to re-assess the reasons for the Smith defeat. They remembered that Walter Lippmann in 1925 had chided those who too hastily assumed that all opposition to Smith must be based on his religion, and they discovered that one Catholic writer of the period had said that what really moved some of Smith's opponents "most profoundly" was that "he was 'New York minded'."

Tammany and Wall Street, from the remote perspective of the delta farm or the crossroads store or the mountain hamlet, looked very much like the same thing. And no amount of explanation by a liberal historian or political scientist could have convinced rural and small-town folk that city-machine graft is somehow socially constructive whereas stock-market graft is by comparison socially regressive—popular as this view has since become in historical essays, novels (particularly Edwin O'Connor's *The Last Hurrah*), and civics textbooks. On the contrary, "the East," by which people in the hinterland meant the East's urban areas rather than the decaying farms, spruce forests, ponds, and hills that remained of Thoreau's East, was seen *in toto* as a parasite consuming the fruit of the productive toil of the rest of the nation. It was, as Bryan called it, "the Enemy's country."

The unfairness of that image in no way detracted from its vividness, and politicians of the day attempted to reckon with it. One such attempt was the now all-but-forgotten presidential candidacy of Senator Thomas J. Walsh of Montana, who, as an Irish Democrat but also a Westerner, a Catholic but also a Dry, was free from the stereotype of urban corruption that clung to Governor Smith. The Montanan was best known nationally for the prosecution of the Teapot Dome investigations, and as a business broker in New York who admired Walsh put it, "Al Smith is the head of an organization which has collected much more graft than that involved in the Teapot Dome." J. Leonard Bates and others have shown that Walsh got more credit in the Teapot Dome affair than he has historically deserved, and Smith himself had demonstrated that an honest man could rise through Tammany; but still, as Mark Sullivan wrote in his syndicated newspaper column for April 1, 1928, should Walsh be elected President, "no one would suspect a private wire to Tammany Hall."

But in the California presidential primary, that graveyard of more than one American candidacy, Smith trounced Walsh in 1928. As a matter of fact, the consensus of historians is coming to be that the governor was an unusually strong Democratic candidate in a presidential year when the country would almost certainly have gone for Hoover in any case; Samuel Lubell has summed up the magnitude of the New Yorker's national political achievement in one memorable line: "Before the Roosevelt Revolution there was an Al Smith Revolution." Still, it was something of a revolution in a vacuum, for part of the tragedy of this talented inhabitant of the Empire State was that he never quite learned to take the rest of the country seriously.

In an informal campaign biography of Smith, published in 1927, Henry F. Pringle told of a journalist who asked the New York executive in an interview for some comment on public affairs which might be of interest to readers in states west of the Mississippi, and was taken aback when Al retorted: "What states *are* west of the Mississippi?" This is of course a familiar and perennial New York attitude. "After New York it's all Bridgeport," as they say in show business; and at a different point along the social spectrum from Al Smith his contemporary Ford Madox Ford confessed in 1927 that except for trips to Europe he "ventures outside the charmed circle of Gotham with the timorous sensation of one inserting his toe into the sea in order to test its temperature." *New York Is Not America,* Ford entitled these musings, and the converse was also true, he thought: fleeing the cultural confinement of Main Street, "the American who settles in New York becomes at once an ex-American."

In Governor Smith the rejection of the America that was not New York did not go *that* far, but it went far enough that David Burner, in one study of the brown derby campaign of 1928, accused the "Gotham Cockney," as he called Smith, of "an exclusionist provinciality unequalled even during the bids of William Jennings Bryan." Nor was it even a liberal provincialism; Robert Moses later testified that "Smith thought about economics in many ways like a Southern conservative"—or, he might have added, like a mildly progressive Republican such as Herbert Hoover, who *was* born west of the Mississippi. Professor Burner agrees with this estimate by Moses: "On economic issues the Governor was far less adventurous than William Jennings Bryan had been early in the twenties."

Indeed, in a sense the failure of Alfred E. Smith was the failure of William Jennings Bryan, but in reverse; each man was repulsed by the other's most devoted constituents, and each had loyal followers who loved him for the enemies he had made. In their one direct encounter at Madison Square Garden in 1924, when Smith's cause was most hopeless and Bryan's most dubious, Bryan was roundly booed by his New York audience, but the Nebraskan had also been booed by Tammany's cohorts at other Democratic national conventions when his cause had been a better one. In his very first campaign of 1896, when Bryan almost single-handedly came within a half-million votes of beating McKinley's patronage, Hanna's organization, and the GOP's millions (here the present writer follows Mrs. Cabot Lodge's judgment on that election, not the historian Carl Degler's), the oratorical magic seems to have worked almost everywhere except in New York City; there, the normally Democratic New York *World* described the Commoner's Manhattan appearance in contemptuous language that makes the partisanship of twentieth-century newpapers sound tame by comparison. In perspective, the man's later attempts to defend the values of his midwestern upbringing, even its biblical fundamentalism, become more humanly understandable.

Who will now say, for example, that Tammany's preferred choice as a presidential nominee in 1912 would have been better than Bryan's? Indeed, who now remembers him? And in 1916, when in spite of their breach over foreign policy Bryan again campaigned for Woodrow Wilson, concentrating on the states where his own personal following was strongest—crucial states the Democratic ticket needed in order to win—the orator from the Platte afterward interpreted Wilson's victory over Hughes to mean that "the scepter has passed from New York" in an election won "by the West and the South without the aid or consent of the East." "This mood," comments Lawrence W.

Levine, "which was echoed by numerous progressive Democrats throughout the country, is important for an understanding of the difficulties the Democratic party was to face in the Twenties."

We could understand those difficulties more clearly were it not for the caricature that has passed for a portrait of Bryan among American historians and men of letters. The fashion was set soon after Bryan's death by Paxton Hibben in his biography *The Peerless Leader,* itself a monument to the Twenties in its "debunking" style, and it continued well into the Fifties in *Inherit the Wind,* a stage and screen dramatization of the Scopes Trial, whose authors felt obliged to invent a subplot having no basis in history, making the Bryan character not merely ignorant and pompous but a moral monster as well. If the textbooks sometimes treated him favorably, as in Morison and Commager's summary sentence, "Bryan was the link between Andrew Jackson and Franklin D. Roosevelt," the monographs until only a few years ago presented Bryan instead as the link between Jackson and Barry Goldwater, the latter being viewed with a bristling and quite unacademic hostility.

But surely there is something to be said for a political leader of whom Mr. Justice Frankfurter, an astringently rational man, in his reminiscence for the Columbia University Oral History Project in 1953 could still say "Bryan was for me with reference to public affairs what some actor or actress is to an adolescent girl." With the new studies of Bryan in the Sixties by Lawrence W. Levine, Paolo Coletta, and Paul W. Glad, the balance began to be redressed. In particular Professor Levine's *Defender of the Faith,* which focused on the Great Commoner's last and most controversial ten years, flatly contradicts the previously usual image of Bryan during the Twenties. In view of the general demoralization in the ranks of the postwar progressives, Levine writes, it would be quite understandable had Bryan abandoned the humanitarian causes of his youth—"but, in fact, no such abandonment took place."

"Have faith in mankind," Bryan cried in 1922, in the midst

of the apathy, cynicism, and selfishness of the undistinguished regime of Warren Harding. ". . . It is easier to-day for one to be helpful to the whole world than it was a few centuries ago to be helpful to the inhabitants of a single valley." What is surprising about these lines is that they occur in a book by Bryan, *In His Image,* the main purpose of which was to refute the theory of evolution; and this in turn suggests not only that the historical portrait of William Jennings Bryan needed to be redrawn but also that our picture of his religious milieu requires a few fresh brushstrokes as well.

The theory of "culture-lag" covered a multitude of sins in the Twenties, as in fact it still does. Although the prospect for religion as a whole was not invariably treated as "the future of an illusion," that of Fundamentalism—the belief in the literal inerrancy of Scripture professed by men like Bryan—almost always was, and later generations of historians and other intellectuals have inherited and perpetuated the stereotype. Concluding his very useful study of *The Fundamentalist Controversy,* published in 1954, Norman Furniss wrote: "The men and women who are concerned for the cause of intellectual freedom in mid-century America are aroused by other threats than those represented by the stragglers of the once-potent fundamentalist movement." In an essay intended for use in general survey courses in American history, completed just before his untimely death in 1964, Furniss made the point even more emphatically: "After 1925 the fundamentalist movement began to falter; and by 1930, it had lost national importance." This assumption has colored most of what has been written about Fundamentalism, at least by non-Fundamentalists, ever since.

But many college freshmen in the Fifties and Sixties were still coming into more than one state university's biological sciences courses armed against Darwinist teachings by systematic Lutheran, Baptist, Christian Reformed, sometimes Roman Catholic or even Orthodox Jewish counterinstruction. Sydney Ahlstrom, in a paper read to the American Society of Church History in 1957, hazarded a guess that Fundamentalism and "that popular piety usually associated with Norman Vincent Peale" between them must account for "at least half of America's Christian non-Roman Catholic church-membership." Louis Gasper has traced the vicissitudes of both "moderate" and "extremist" Fundamentalism since 1930 in *The Fundamentalist Movement* (1963), and in compiling material for a reappraisal of Fundamentalism during 1964–65, the present writer turned up new specimens in abundance merely by following the public record. The cliché that Fundamentalism somehow "fell apart" after the Scopes Trial—against evidence like the television presence of Billy Graham and others—is attributable mainly to the fact that in the normal course of things academic intellectuals do not meet and converse with many Fundamentalists, just as the lingering belief in some Republican circles that Roosevelt and the New Deal were a temporary aberration from which we will all return to Normalcy one day is attributable mainly to the fact that in the normal course of things such Republicans meet and converse chiefly with other Republicans.

Charles Y. Glock and Rodney Stark have given sociological foundation to the foregoing line of reasoning. Within a parish of one of the broad "mainstream" churches, they argue, the orthodox communicants are likely to remain unaware of the liberalism of their fellow members "because the people they know in the congregation, their friends, do share" their conservative beliefs, and conversely the liberals, tending to find their social contacts and outlets elsewhere than in the church, and thus "not being linked into the congregation by friendship bonds, may remain largely unaware of the fundamentalist segment of the congregation." The writer would only add from personal observation that the sudden awakening from this state of blissful mutual ignorance can be a shock to both parties.

The Fundamentalists *did*, in the main, lose control of the institutional and public-relations machinery of the established Protestant denominations during the Twenties, at least in the

Northeast, but where Fundamentalism since Bryan's time has gone can be seen in any American city today. William G. McLoughlin has warned against accepting liberal Protestantism's (self-interested?) evaluation of these other, non-"mainstream" churches as "minor," "backward," or "ecstatic"; on the contrary, the new pietistic Fundamentalism as it had taken shape since the mid-Thirties was in fact "a second wing of Protestantism in America." As in the Sixties, so in the Twenties, in order to grasp fully the significance of Fundamentalism it is necessary to see it as a powerful creed having vitality for millions of adherents rather than as a cranky, marginal belief doomed to a speedy extinction.

Still, do not Fundamentalism's rural antecedents support the culture-lag hypothesis, since the United States from the Twenties through the Sixties was becoming increasingly urbanized? "Fundamentalism," writes William E. Leuchtenburg, "made sense to men in isolated rural areas still directly dependent on nature for their livelihood; they distrusted human capacity and relied on divine intervention, because it had been their own experience that men had to rely on the rains for the crops and were all but helpless when disease struck." As agronomy and medicine and mechanization advanced, it would have been logical to expect such a religion to retreat—except for the fact that Fundamentalism's appeal was not limited to rural America.

In a paper read at the 1965 session of the American Historical Association, Ernest R. Sandeen concluded: "Fundamentalism originated in the northeastern part of this continent in metropolitan areas and cannot be explained as a part of the populist movement, agrarian protest or the Southern mentality." And McLoughlin reminds us that "in 1925, contrary to general belief, [Fundamentalism's] leadership and dynamic force came from its urban adherents." It was from a New York City pulpit that the Reverend John Roach Straton thundered at the evolutionists and at Al Smith (and at Sunday baseball) during the

Twenties, and there were effective Fundamentalist ministries in those years in Boston and Philadelphia and Chicago as well as in California, Kansas, and Tennessee. This is not to deny a natural kinship between the old-time religion and the rural mind; for all that it was exaggerated by the metropolitan press the Scopes Trial had *some* symbolical reality. It is, rather, to remind ourselves that one can be "ruralist" by adoption as well as by inheritance. One does not have to be born on a ranch to enjoy a "Western," which millions of Easterners patently do, and similarly one did not have to be an old-timer to accept the old-time religion.

Into old-timer politics also one can be naturalized as well as born; witness the allegiance to Senator Goldwater down through 1964 on the part of well-fed and under-exercised suburban youths even less plausible as rugged frontiersmen than their hero, who at least looked good on a horse. But since there was a notable upsurge of Fundamentalist political discourse specifically in connection with the 1964 presidential campaign, this almost irresistibly suggests another favorite historical stereotype of Fundamentalism: that it is nothing more than the religious version of right-wing secular politics. Ralph Roy in his biting account *Apostles of Discord,* a study of rightist "hate" groups of the early Fifties, documented the persistence and pervasiveness of this connection, such that many warriors in the anti-evolution crusade of the Twenties remained active in anticommunist (and other) crusades of more recent years; and William Leuchtenburg's account of the Twenties included a chapter on Ku Kluxism, anti-immigrantism, Prohibition, and the Scopes Trial—all lumped together as "Political Fundamentalism."

Yet the pivotal figure in the Scopes Trial was William Jennings Bryan, and Bryan, as Willard H. Smith and Lawrence Levine have shown, retained more of a "Social Gospel"—that is, in secular terms, "liberal"—orientation than he has usually been given credit for. In 1919, for example, Bryan urged the Christian Church not to ignore the problem of corporate monopoly;

it must be the Church's task "to protect the God-made man from the man-made giant." And throughout the half-decade of the Twenties into which the Commoner survived, he continued to excoriate the churches for their seeming indifference to such issues as profiteering, tax exploitation, industrial injustice, and international anarchy. There are obvious objections which can be raised to this kind of religion, but they are of a radically different kind from those usually lodged against William Jennings Bryan and against Fundamentalism.

Much Fundamentalist thought in fact was neither "liberal" nor "conservative," but apolitical if not antipolitical; the pessimism toward society at large became so profound that the believer sought redemption *from* it, not *of* it. "Weary with the conflicts of the world, one goes into the Church to seek refreshment for the soul," wrote J. Gresham Machen, a Fundamentalist leader of the Twenties; ". . . alas, too often, one finds only the turmoil of the world." Activists may be tempted to see in this attitude a kind of conservatism by default, and defenders of the *status quo* have at times been only too happy to see the Church withdraw from involvement with and judgment upon the World; but among those—liberals as well as conservatives— who feel that modern man has become excessively politicized, Machen's appeal may strike a more responsive chord. Donald Meyer has argued that the churchly liberals themselves were going to realize one day that the real conflict within the soul of twentieth-century man was not between moral (liberal?) man and immoral (conservative?) society but between, in Meyer's terms, "concrete man" and "abstract society"; and therefore, "the final upshot of the social gospel was that the gospel had to be more personal."

But this was to move the argument up to a level at which only the most sophisticated of Fundamentalists—a J. Gresham Machen, trained at Marburg and Göttingen, but not a Bryan— could have followed it. And in any event the showdown between Fundamentalism and Modernism in the Twenties was not directly over political doctrines either Left or Right, but over the theory of evolution. Whether Fundamentalism be at bottom "liberal" or "conservative" or neither of these in the political sense, was it not skewed in the direction of intolerance (a trait the liberal is prone to define as conservative, and vice versa) by its innate hostility to science?

There is obviously some justice in this view, as the tactics of the anti-evolution crusade made evident. But to accept it fully would be to overrate the persuasive power of the scientific tenets to which Fundamentalism was opposed. There was and is a widely held belief that the decrees of science are self-executing: pit the Bible and the *Origin of Species* against each other in fair and open combat and the truth, whatever it may be, will out. Hence any man other than one of Mencken's "gaping primates" who had once been exposed to the theory of evolution, unless deterred by considerations of convenience or opportunism—his neighbors might all be Fundamentalists, or he might be an Elmer Gantry—must accept the scientific truth and cease forthwith to be a Fundamentalist. The trouble with this kind of reasoning is that it expects too much of pedagogy, informal or formal.

In the Twenties as later—compare the "two cultures" controversy—the scientific *method* was rarely taught systematically to the nonscientist. The textbook used by John Thomas Scopes in the high school at Dayton, Tennessee, is a case in point. One paragraph of Hunter's *Civic Biology* was subheaded "The Doctrine of Evolution"; a sentence within it began with the words "Geology teaches . . . . ," and the sentence following commenced with "The great English scientist, Charles Darwin . . . ." The student was, in short, being taught a dogma based on authority: "Science says" in place of "Thus saith the Lord." A page or so later there appeared a chart of "the evolutionary tree," containing the various animal phyla in simplified form, and the pupil was told in the caption: "Copy this diagram in your notebook. Explain it as well as you can"—an intellectual process not markedly different from the way Sunday-school children learned their Bible verses and the Catechism.

To be sure, after the launching of Sputnik I, efforts were going to be made in America to purge secondary-school science texts both of this sort of thing and also of information and concepts that were simply out of date. But Sir Charles Snow in his *Two Cultures* essay (1959) ominously warned that the gap between the language of science and the language of the humanities (and of "common sense") might have opened so far as to have become unbridgeable—and many a literary intellectual, judging from his uncritical enthusiasm for F. R. Leavis's critique of Snow, seems at times not to *want* to understand science, in as cranky and closed-minded a way as any Fundamentalist.

But all that lay far in the future at the time of *Tennessee* v. *John Thomas Scopes*. As a matter of fact, the Twenties were a low point in the scientists' own efforts to understand and verify the process of evolution, and some of the more perceptive of the champions of orthodoxy knew this. With a debater's killer-instinct, Alfred W. McCann in the first chapter of his bombastic tract *God—or Gorilla?* attacked the credibility of "Piltdown Man," and to the chagrin of the Darwinists that particular fossil was in due course shown to be a fraud. In a symposium of reminiscences of the Scopes Trial forty years afterward, Lamont C. Cole, chairman of the Zoology Department at Cornell, commented on his father's deposition as an expert witness at the trial: "As I compare that statement with the account of human evolution found in a leading college textbook of zoology published more than a quarter of a century later, I am impressed by the firm and definite conclusions that could be drawn in 1925 from the then scanty fossil evidence." Since scientific hypotheses come and go, Fundamentalists were therefore able to argue, why should anyone accept an evolutionary theory which might be supplanted tomorrow, in preference to "the Faith once delivered to the saints"?

Of course few of the Fundamentalists—and few of the Modernists, one must add in all fairness—could have appreciated a critique with the dialectical subtlety of Louis T. More's *The Dogma of Evolution;* nor would most of them have been aware of the confession of the British geneticist Sir William Bateson before the American Association for the Advancement of Science that "discussions of evolution" had come "to an end primarily because it was obvious that no progress was being made. . . . Variation of many kinds, often considerable, we daily witness, but no origin of species" (*Science,* January 20, 1922). If rural folk in particular distrusted the theory of evolution, it would not have been because they found it "unnatural"—any farmer who has bred stock knows there is *something* in the idea!—or because they knew how incomplete the scientists' own knowledge was, especially with regard to fossil man, but rather that the articulate propaganda for the theory was emanating from city pulpits, city universities, and city textbook publishers.

Thus in the last analysis we return to the hypothesis of rural-urban conflict in order to interpret Fundamentalism. McLoughlin's and Sandeen's point about the urban genesis and leadership of that movement (for example, the men of the Moody Bible Institute in Chicago) remains well taken, but we must not forget that people who move to the city do not necessarily cease to be country people. On one occasion the flamboyant evangelist Aimee Semple McPherson, who represented a successful fusion of Fundamentalism's rejection of the World, the Flesh, and the Devil with a nascent Hollywood culture's triumphant affirmation of all three, walked onto the stage of her Four-Square Gospel temple in Los Angeles carrying a full milk pail and asked her hearers how many of them had ever lived on a farm; Carey McWilliams, in his essay for *The Aspirin Age* (1949), reported that "the entire audience stood up."

George E. Mowry has rightly asserted of the Twenties: "It was during those years that the country first became urban, particularly in the cast of its mind, in its ideals, and in its folkways." The census statistics for 1920 convincingly support that judgment. But against this we must keep in mind the persistence of ruralism from the Twenties down through the Sixties, often at a more highbrow level than that of Fundamentalism: *The New York Times* editorialist wrote his nature column, the junior senator from New York went mountain climbing, and the sometime Columbia professor and *Nation* drama critic moved to Arizona to observe the behavior of birds and lizards. Even an urban socialist thoroughly attuned to industrial society, Harvey Swados, has confessed, "I am of the city but not for it, for the countryside but not of it"; and on a day in early June of 1965 that seeker after consensus Lyndon B. Johnson paused from deploying warships and jet planes, the spearheads of an urban-industrial technology, to recall the hills of his West Texas boyhood: "Sometimes, in the highest councils of the nation, in this house [the White House], I sit back and I can almost feel that rough, unyielding, sticky clay soil between my fingers."

"The city stalks the country," a country poet has written, and for psychic purposes almost any kind of American can be a countryman at one time or another. In our first chapter we touched upon the ambivalence of the archetypal Henry Ford as between the future and the past; this was also, of course, an ambivalence as between town and country. In the words of the Nevins and Hill study, "Ford the countryman, the son of farming people, the child of Springwell Township lately wrested from the forest," who in fact had gone off to Detroit as a youth because he greatly preferred tinkering with machinery to farming, "was projected to leadership of the industrial and urban age"—but all his life the man who had done so much to bring the city to the farm faced emotionally in both directions.

Frank Lloyd Wright, too, although dedicated to full use of the materials and construction methods appropriate to the Machine Age, wrote in 1910 of the "ignoble parasitism" on European architectural models by Americans as being "more characteristic of the Eastern citizen on the cinder-strip than [of] the Western citizen of the great prairies"; and at the beginning of the

Twenties he was turning from the style of the "prairie houses" he had built in his beloved Midwest to forms even less urban in their inspiration, houses in California and Arizona which recalled Mayan temples in the jungles of Yucatán or the natural topography of the desert itself. It is only necessary to compare Wright's work in the Twenties with Weimar Germany's *Bauhaus* and its uncompromisingly mechanistic and aseptic canons of design to be reminded that throughout a long and vigorous career the prairie architect reminisced of boyhood summers on Grandfather's farm, complete with buzzing bees and new-mown hay.

Frank Lloyd Wright wrote and spoke of his anti-urban organicism as "democracy in overalls"; and Hiram Wesley Evans, Imperial Wizard of the Ku Klux Klan, in a much-anthologized statement of 1926, complained against encroachment of the new urban civilization on behalf of the " 'rubes' and 'hicks' and 'drivers of second-hand Fords'," linking these people emotionally with the democrats in overalls who had been associated with the political fortunes of Jackson and Lincoln and Bryan. Properly, the Klansmen too should be seen as "ruralist," rather than necessarily as "rural." In a study of the Ku Klux Klan in Texas during the Twenties, Charles C. Alexander showed that "the Klan achieved its greatest strength and its most notable successes in the booming cities," among "Texans who found themselves living in a rapidly changing urban environment but clinging to the values of their rural background."

Our sympathy quickly cools when we learn that it was only "the Nordic American" for whom Imperial Wizard Evans spoke; the common men enrolled in the Ku Klux Klan acknowledged no solidarity with such other categories of common men as, for example, immigrants, Negroes, Jews, Catholics, or northeastern city-dwellers. Taking this fact together with Henry Ford's private police, his hostility to labor unions, or his anti-Semitism, and also with Frank Lloyd Wright's apotheosis in fiction by Ayn Rand as a hero of the ultra-Right, it would be very easy to fall

G

into the familiar stereotyped view that urban-rural conflict reduces to a struggle between humane civilization and something very like Fascism. Nevertheless, the present writer submits that to do so would be seriously to misread the history of the Twenties, if not of modern America as a whole.

In saying this, he dissents from a strong trend within his guild. Morton and Lucia White, in their luminous essay *The Intellectual versus the City: From Thomas Jefferson to Frank Lloyd Wright,* described an anti-urban bias endemic among American thinkers, but it is significant that of the dozen persons whom they discuss in some depth only one or perhaps two can be classified essentially as historians. The historiographic tendency in recent years has been to assume, not merely that the traditional American myth of agrarian virtue pitted against metropolitan vice is untrue, but that something very like the reverse is true: namely, that the city in America has had to fight to sustain its humane values against the onslaughts of a mean-spirited and narrow-minded ruralism. In many a monograph, whatever was narrow, corrupt, and vicious in rural life has been deemed typical, and whatever was tolerant, large-minded, and rational in city life has also been considered typical. But there is real danger that in revising the agrarian myth we shall end with the disconcerting discovery that our heroes and villains have simply changed places, to the detriment of historical insight.

A single crucial example will illustrate the point. We have already observed that the high school science textbook out of which John Thomas Scopes taught the theory of evolution was not remarkably scientific; what is even more ironical, considering that the American Civil Liberties Union was in Scopes's corner at the trial, is that some of the doctrines it contained were positively illiberal. Two pages after the paragraph on evolution appeared a paragraph on "The Races of Man," and the author, describing the "five races or varieties of man, each very different from the others," capped the list with "the highest type of all, the Caucasians, represented by the civilized white inhabitants of Europe and America." Thus if a high school student had been emancipated from religious superstition by reading this textbook's account of evolution, he ran the risk of becoming bound in the more lethal superstition of race. The fact that the Scopes Trial took place in the rural South, which did not need or care to learn its racism out of a textbook, must be paired with the fact that a national supplier of schoolbooks, with headquarters in New York, Cincinnati, and Chicago, in publishing Hunter's *Civic Biology* was furthering the propagation *en masse* of a doctrine which it would be not unfair to refer to as "urban racism."

Urban (or "highbrow") racism was if anything more insidious than rural (or "lowbrow") racism since it was more developed and systematic. It had a long pedigree in intellectual America, far antedating the Twenties. Jurgen Herbst quotes Professor John W. Burgess of Columbia, speaking before the Kaiser in Berlin in 1907, as having said "Uncle Sam does not want such rabble for citizens" as Slavs, Czechs, Hungarians, and South Italians. The British historian Edward A. Freeman would have agreed; he wrote in 1882 that America's social problems might be solved if only "every Irishman [were to] kill a Negro and be hanged for it." And the First World War only interrupted and dampened, but by no means extinguished, in America a rhetoric of "Nordic," "Aryan," sometimes "Anglo-Saxon" racial supremacy fully as assured and dogmatic as anything then heard in Germany.

Textbooks of the Twenties (and for long afterward) were filled with descriptions of those classic degenerate families the Jukeses and the Kallikaks, accounts which by ignoring environmental and stressing "instinctual" factors seemed to give the thesis of biological inheritance of superior and inferior mental and even moral traits a scientific rationale. The newly developed and only half-understood "intelligence tests" used on Army recruits in the recent war seemed to give this racist thesis real statistical substance, and attracted to it men of the stature of Edward L. Thorndike and Lewis Terman, psychologists; Henry Pratt Fairchild, professor of sociology at New York University; Paul Popenoe, editor of the *Journal of Heredity;* and many others. "It is natural," writes Thomas F. Gossett, "that in the histories of [the Twenties] the views of the extremists have been accorded more attention, but it was mainly the academic writers on racial differences who made racism respectable"—and a good many of those academic writers held tenured chairs in urban universities.

Our suggestion that the substitution of a half-understood Darwinism for a half-understood Bible could have led to an intellectualized racism is not fanciful. Henry Fairfield Osborn, director of the American Museum of Natural History where he aroused the wrath of Fundamentalists in 1926 with a vivid exhibit on the Age of Man, and author of a popular evolutionist tract *The Earth Speaks to Bryan,* agreed to testify at the Scopes Trial as an expert witness for Science; but in other quarters Osborn was better known for his campaigns for immigration restriction to keep the population balance in the United States predominantly Nordic. And when Walter Lippmann, for example, took issue with men of high scientific standing and denied that mental ability was largely a matter of inheritance, the Harvard psychology professor William MacDougall declared that Lippmann was "denying also the theory of organic evolution, and he should come out openly on the side of Mr. Bryan."

"A man did not need to read an article or book on the biological, anthropological, psychological, or sociological aspects of race in order to participate in a race riot," Gossett concedes. "Still, ideas have a way of trickling down." And if general historical and scientific information had its popularizers, as we noted in a previous chapter, so did "scientific" racism. There were Madison Grant's *The Passing of the Great Race,* Harvard geneticist Edwin East's *Heredity and Human Affairs,* and *The Rising Tide of Color* and other such works by Lothrop Stoddard, whose writings were on the whole favorably reviewed, by *The New York Times* and the *Bookman* among others. For that matter there were the fictional accounts like *The Red Napoleon* (previously discussed in a different context) and the British thriller that chronicled the career of *The Insidious Dr. Fu-Manchu,* whose untiring efforts to upset "the balance which a wise providence has adjusted between the white and yellow races" went into its fifth American printing in 1920 and whose exploits would still be selling briskly in paperback and on film in the Sixties, when Americans were confronting a real China even more formidable, if rather less colorful, than the one created in the vivid imagination of Sax Rohmer.

In one sense at least, the racism of the Twenties was far more vicious in its effect than that of the Sixties. The latter, apart from a few feeble tracts by professors in browbeaten Southern universities, had no intellectual defense, and when challenged had to retreat into blind irrationality or frankly-acknowledged prejudice; so a tale like that of the evil Chinese doctor could be taken and read for what it was, a fantasy. But racism in the Twenties, apart from the pioneering anthropological studies of race by Alês Hrdlicka and Franz Boas which would in due course undermine and discredit the concept, seemed to have the thoughtful, documented sanction of competent scholarship. As a result, racial bias was strengthened throughout the formal Establishment. Jewish quotas were established for admission to universities, particularly in the East, during this period, and Ellery Sedgwick, editor of the venerable *Atlantic Monthly,* was reluctant to publish the essays which were to become *The Modern Temper* on the ground that "the attitude is typical of the Jewish intellectual." Mr. Krutch, an Aryan native of Kentucky descended from a German refugee of 1848 named Krützsch, commented in his autobiography: "If blond Nordics (even though not Bostonian) were entertaining any such thoughts as mine there could be no telling what the world would come to."

Of course it was not only in Establishment circles that racist attitudes could be found in American cities during the Twenties. Discrimination by a college fraternity or a literary magazine or a summer resort might be an imposition and an inconvenience, but discrimination by a trade union, for example, could strike at survival itself. Irving Bernstein in *The Lean Years,* a history of the American worker during the Twenties and early Thirties, noted that technically the American Federation of Labor banned racial discrimination, but that in practice the power of admission to union membership rested with the internationals. "The Boilermakers and Machinists, for example, got around [the ban] simply by incorporating a racial clause in their rituals, binding members to propose only white workmen for membership." C. W. Chesnutt, testifying before a Senate subcommittee in 1928, was blunt: "I make the charge baldly that the labor unions of the United States, broadly speaking, are unfriendly to Negro labor, and I challenge them to prove the contrary."

Still more disquieting, in the light of developments since the Twenties, was the emergence of overtly racist attitudes among urban Negroes themselves. Marcus Garvey, a Jamaican who came to the United States with a "Back-to-Africa" plan for American Negroes, praised Warren Harding for a speech delivered in Birmingham in 1921 against racial amalgamation, and later supported a back-to-Africa bill sponsored by the unspeakably race-baiting Senator Theodore G. Bilbo of Mississippi; Negro pride, the mirror-image of the white man's, demanded that the races separate. Garvey ruled his Universal Negro Improvement Association, writes John Hope Franklin, "with the assistance of one Potentate and one Supreme Deputy Potentate" and such orders as "the Knights of the Nile, the Knights of the Distinguished Service Order of Ethiopia, and the Dukes of the Niger and of Uganda"—not so very far from the world of Grand Dragons, Great Titans, King Kleagles, Kludds, Klaliffs, and Klokards presided over by Hiram Wesley Evans; and the Klan, for the complementary opposite of Garvey's reasons, openly supported the Garvey movement. "Garveyism was for the most part decisively repudiated by the Negro intellectuals" of the Harlem Renaissance, concedes E. David Cronon in his study of Marcus Garvey *Black Moses,* but this "escapist program of chauvinistic Negro nationalism" (as Cronon calls it) seems nevertheless to have had a wide popular following among Harlem Negroes: "To know Garvey is, in a sense, to understand the Negro world of the Twenties."

Racism then, like other forms of man's inhumanity to man in the Twenties, was found on metropolitan campuses as well as in rural high schools, in labor unions as well as in business associations, in fashionable suburbs as well as in small towns (what right had Darien to complain about Gopher Prairie?), and above all in the city as well as in the country. And unlike some of the other social phenomena characteristic of the Twenties this one has unfortunately not become dated or quaint. It survived into the Sixties, not only in the race riot and the slum ghetto and the segregated building-trades union, but also, down to 1965, on the lawbooks, in the immigration legislation written into statute in the Twenties.

Less drastic in operation than the laws for the sterilization of defectives enacted during the same period, which were constitutionally upheld by Mr. Justice Holmes on the ground that society should have the right to "prevent those who are manifestly unfit from continuing their kind" (*Buck* v. *Bell,* 274 U.S. 200, 1927), this legislation was equally eugenist in intent. Americans could plausibly have argued that a declining industrial labor force had no room for foreign workers even in a time of prosperity, and in a time of depression Franklin Roosevelt (or one of his ghost-writers) was to declare: "We are not able to invite the immigration from Europe to share our endless plenty. We are now providing a drab living for our own people." But the "quota" system, whereby the *proportions* of the various nationalities (or, in the more extreme view, "races") as they existed in the United States were to be maintained unchanged in what little immigration would still be permitted, clearly favored the "superior" ethnic stocks from the north and west of Europe, and reduced to a trickle the flow from the "inferior" south and east.

An exception perforce to the general policy, owing to American colonialism, was immigration from the Philippine Islands, which multiplied ten times during the decade 1920–30; but, comments Maldwyn Allen Jones in closing a chapter on the demand for restriction in his study of immigration in American history, the whole melancholy history of the immigration controversy prior to the Twenties was now repeated in miniature, with anti-Filipino demonstrations in California and Washington and a not entirely disinterested drive for Philippine independence. Both in deciding to write off the Philippine military campaign of 1899–1902 as a bad job and set the islands free, and in enacting so fundamental a reversal of America's historic policy toward the foreign-born as the national origins system represented, the Congress of the United States did not in any clear-cut way divide on "liberal" and "conservative" lines.

If the Senate had heard racist arguments for the immigration-restriction bill it passed in 1897 couched in the Beacon Hill accents of the elder Henry Cabot Lodge, a conservative to his fingertips, it had also heard the almost equally conservative President Grover Cleveland strike down that bill with one of his typically plain-spoken vetoes. Similar bills had been blocked by the determined actions of the more-or-less conservative Taft and the more-or-less liberal Wilson. Among the "progressives," a term whose definition is beginning to pose an even greater problem for historians of modern America than "liberal" and "conservative," immigration restriction had long been an important objective, and William Leuchtenburg has pointed out that when the moment of truth came in 1924, not a single "progressive" vote in Congress was cast against the bill. Was this the Ku Klux Klan mentality in action, defending the purity of an agrarian America against alien contamination? We have been told over and over again by modern historians of Progressivism that the animus of that reform movement, by contrast with Populism, was urban.

In summation, bigotry and intolerance in the Twenties were not a rural monopoly, and equally a case could be made that humanitarianism and enlightenment—compare the metropolitan Hearst newspapers with the bucolic Emporia (Kansas) *Gazette*—were not an urban one. It was as one country boy to another that the *Gazette*'s editor, William Allen White, having just finished reading *Main Street* aloud with Mrs. White, wrote to Sinclair Lewis on November 23, 1920, "to tell you what a noble thing you have done" and declared that if he were a millionaire he "would go and bribe the legislature of Kansas to make 'Main Street' compulsory reading in the public schools." The Sage of Emporia seems also to have been on reasonably genial terms with that passionate antiruralist H. L. Mencken— data which do not fit the stereotype either of the city stalking the country or of the country strangling the city. Then, too, if Richard Hofstadter is right in saying that "life-adjustment educators would do anything in the name of science except encourage children to study it," it may well be that all the anti-evolution statutes threatened or enacted in all of rural or rural-minded America put together have not blighted as many budding young minds as have the dedicated disciples of the "new education" who in the Twenties came charging out upon the land from one metropolitan teachers' college.

The foregoing analysis has been intended as a correction of the historian's tendency to dwell upon the regressive features of American rural culture, and to neglect the equally unsavory aspects of the metropolitan past—a tendency that Mario S. DePillis, in a paper read before the Mississippi Valley Historical Association in 1965, deplored as "the chauvinism of the urban historians, who seem to believe that for urban history to rise, rural history must fall." But in understanding the rural-urban polarity in America, for the Twenties or for any other time, nothing is gained if we merely reverse the plus and minus signs once again. Town and country as unmitigated opposites—the world of *Main Street,* let us say, as against the world of *Manhattan Transfer*—can be understood historically only from a point of view which transcends them. In the rapidly urbanizing environment of the Sixties and Seventies, this may be more easily said than done, but the effort is nevertheless necessary.

On making the effort we may find that the polarity is not as absolute as it has sometimes appeared to be. In a thoughtful review of the Whites' *The Intellectual versus the City,* William H. Jordy suggested that the anti-urban writers in America have embraced values that are not really small-town or rural at all: "If the city has been attacked, have intellectuals been substantially kinder to farming?" What they really wanted was a "metropolitan arcadianism, which differs from the folksiness of small-town attitudes in its emphasis on civilized values and a fundamentally complex social organization"—and very often the "agrarian" Utopias have come down in reality to no more than "the suburban community, but without the chore of daily commuting."

Leo Marx has another name for the tragic response of American men of letters to the machine's invasion of the garden: "complex pastoralism." Without the complexity, the intellectual's pastoralism could become grotesque, as when the Rhode Island fantasy-writer and antiquarian Howard Phillips Lovecraft first saw the skyline of New York in 1922 and told his Manhattan host "that man is like the coral insect—designed to build vast, beautiful, mineral things for the moon to delight in after he is dead." The point of view is as inhumane as anything generated from within Megalopolis, for all its cosmic awe, and one is not surprised to find Lovecraft declaring elsewhere in the same paragraph, "I could not take humanity seriously if I wanted to." It is worth noting that the men who knew Lovecraft best have agreed that it took another and a far more traumatic, even tragic, stay in New York to mature him both as a writer and as a human being—"he came out of it pure gold," one of them declared afterward—even though he did in the end forsake the Babylonian towers on the Hudson for his own "green New England lanes."

As a matter of fact, the most informed misgivings about Megalopolis have always been articulated in Megalopolis itself. *The Commonweal,* published in New York City, inaugurated its second year of publication on May 13, 1925, with a lead editorial on "The Terrible Super-City," prophesying an automated and dehumanized society along the lines made familiar to us by the culture-criticism of more recent years. It is instructive for the reader in the Sixties, fresh from our own discussions of the population explosion, to learn that a Catholic journal in the Twenties could even then have raised the question "whether the limit of numbers permitting the community sense has not already been surpassed"; and although the editorial asked if men could "stem the creation of monster communities with no soul, and work back to groups who know each other," it would be unthinkable to classify this liberal metropolitan weekly as "anti-urban."

But the tragedy of any polar situation is that it becomes almost impossible for such balanced views to prevail. Instead it becomes a choice of Al Smith *or* Bryan, scientism *or* biblicism, immigrant *or* native, Wet *or* Dry, H. L. Mencken *or* Aimee Semple McPherson, Chicago gangster *or* Mississippi lyncher, bohemian *or* philistine. Town and country had found a common voice in America before, as when New York and Philadelphia workingmen rallied to Jackson or when Lincoln the backwoodsman campaigned successfully in the Cooper Union; and they would find it again when a country squire from Hyde Park mastered the city machines and enlisted auto worker and farmer under the same banner. But for the decade of the Twenties, town and country had lost the knack of speaking in concert, and shouted each other down.

To read what some man . . . has said about a great live book, this, which . . . we are all so jubilant over as a splendid way of saving labor, is probably as unstimulating and unfertilizing a process as the human mind can submit to. . . . It sets us all to writing books or judging of them with reference to other books that have already been written and judged, not with immediate reference to truths and thoughts. . . . No; read books themselves, and not men's talk about them. To read a book is to make a friend. To read a review is to be introduced to a passing stranger.

PHILLIPS BROOKS, late Bishop of Massachusetts (1875)

Suggestions for Further Study

This will not be a formal bibliographic essay. The historian Burl Noggle, in the *Journal of American History,* LIII (September, 1966), 299–314, has documented a discussion of "The Twenties: A New Historiographical Frontier" so exhaustively, with footnotes which in turn lead one back to the notes of others, that to go over the same ground here would be in effect to compile a bibliography of a bibliography of bibliographies, an exercise in pedantic futility. The reader in search of an author or title referred to in the text but not discussed here may find what he is looking for by turning to the Index; the writer will use this space instead for what a congressman would call "revising and extending my remarks for the *Record.*"

The first comment is simply that in spite of all the historical monographs discussed in Noggle's essay and in this book there remains a great deal of work to be done on the Twenties. Systematic economic history (except on the Crash itself) is one such area, a gap which is reflected in the text itself. The history of economic theory has been admirably covered by Joseph Dorfman in the

99

fourth volume of *The Economic Mind in American Civilization* (New York, 1959), and there are thorough studies on individual businesses, such as automobiles, in Allan Nevins and Frank Ernest Hill, *Ford: Expansion and Challenge 1915–1933* (New York, 1957) and oil, in Harold F. Williamson and others, *The American Petroleum Industry*, II: *The Age of Energy, 1899–1959* (Evanston, Ill., 1959). Badly needed is the kind of monograph which would pull these two diverse sorts of inquiry together; indeed, really to do justice to this subject would require a book far greater in bulk than the present one.

There are other gaps as well. It is typical, and noteworthy, that the authors of a symposium published in 1964 on *Change and Continuity in Twentieth Century America* when giving examples of the "continuity" tended to find them in the First World War (William E. Leuchtenberg), the Progressive Era (John Braeman), or even the Nineties (Richard Leopold). Allusions to the Twenties in most of these articles were made in passing, as if the Twenties had been an aberration, subordinate to an overall scheme of the twentieth century into which those years did not fit. Significantly, the editors of the Ohio State University Press' "Modern America" series, of which this study in change and continuity was the initial volume, scheduled as the second a collection of similar monographs specifically on the Twenties.

If much work remains to be done on the Twenties, still the past decade has seen a quickening of interest in the period. The catalyst for much of this discussion, as more than one monographist has acknowledged, was Henry F. May, "Shifting Perspectives on the 1920's," *Mississippi Valley Historical Review,* XLIII (1956), 405ff. The student would do well to begin by reading this luminous and literate essay. The present writer has in addition received a powerful conceptual stimulus from Leo Lowenthal's study, "Biographies in Popular Magazines," which is discussed at some length in the text; that article was reprinted without substantial change as "The Triumph of Mass Idols," Chapter IV in *Literature, Popular Culture, and Society* (Englewood Cliffs, N.J., 1961). Neither May nor Lowenthal is, of course, responsible for the particular responses of this writer to their creative influence.

Any hypothesis is subject to critical test. The reader is therefore invited to check the validity of the Lowenthal hypothesis (as used herein) against such contemporary studies of the Twenties as the President's Research Committee on Social Trends, eds., *Recent*

Social Trends in the United States (New York, 1933) and, on a smaller cross-sectional scale, Robert S. Lynd and Helen Merrell Lynd, *Middletown: A Study in American Culture* (New York, 1929). Similarly, the rural-urban polarity of which so much is made in our third chapter must be tested against that social trend of the Twenties which was neither the one pole nor the other; a pioneering and still readable study is H. Paul Douglass, *The Suburban Trend* (New York, 1925). A more recent and polemical discussion is Lewis Mumford, "Suburbia and Beyond," Chapter 16 in *The City in History: Its Origins, Its Transformations, and Its Prospects* (New York, 1961). Constance McLaughlin Green, *American Cities in the Growth of the Nation* (London, 1957), is important for background on particular cities—her account of Detroit is particularly insightful—and the work is free from the "urban chauvinism" of which Mario De Pillis complained (see above, p. 95–96): "the middle years of the twentieth century . . . may constitute the last period of American history in which city influence will overshadow every other in the nation," Mrs. Green quite surprisingly concludes.

An even better way of probing the concrete historical reality out of which all sociological (and historical!) generalizations arise than reading the arguments of scholars is to immerse oneself in the magazines of the Twenties, both the "mass-media" kind studied by Lowenthal and the news-comment-and-culture-criticism sort. Robert B. Luce has judiciously edited a selection from one journal in the latter category, *The New Republic,* entitled *Faces of Five Decades* (New York, 1964); pp. 54–175 deal with the Twenties, and in 1967 the newsmagazine *Time* launched a series of *"Time* Capsules," digesting selected years from its back files. Other such anthologies might be a worthwhile publishing venture, particularly if they excerpted not only those periodicals that have survived into our own time (*New Yorker, Commonweal*) but also, and even more instructively, those that have not (*The Literary Digest, World's Work*). The compendium by Cleveland Amory, *et al.,* from *Vanity Fair* (New York, 1960) was a step in that direction.

Still, useful as such collections are, nothing substitutes for a plunge into the files themselves. The reader is particularly fortunate who has access to bound volumes he can handle physically, without the subtle separation from reality inherent in the use of microfilm. He would do well to vary his diet of dated politics and literary opinion with some sampling of the specialized presses—religious

(*Christian Century, Catholic World*), popular science (*Scientific American*), light satire (the old *Life*), and the like—not neglecting the so-called "little magazines." He should also pay some attention to changing styles in advertisements, layout, typography, and artwork. For the mass-media publications, a useful account of their transformation from the times of the muckrakers to our own day is Theodore Bernard Peterson, *Magazines in the Twentieth Century*, 2d ed. (Urbana, Ill., 1964).

For more formal endeavors in the arts, both "fine" and "lively," there is likewise no substitute for the work itself. The student is urged to read the novel, hear the jazz, see the play, walk through the building. Secondary discussion, particularly technical elucidation (as in Arthur Drexler's brief editorial introduction to *The Drawings of Frank Lloyd Wright* [New York, 1962] or as in explanations of the technique of motion-picture film editing), can be helpful, but it is intrinsically dangerous; even a photograph of a building can editorialize. For the Twenties, it is hard to find a critical tract in any of these fields that is not, in some sense, partisan.

For a particularly extreme example, see almost everything that has been written about Ezra Pound. He and his work were declared "in" by the poetic beau ideal of the Twenties, T. S. Eliot, who dedicated his *Waste Land* to Pound in 1922; "out" by the United States Army, which after Pound's pro-Axis broadcasts from Rome in the Second World War confined him in a detention stockade; "in" by a prize committee of the Library of Congress, and "out" by the *Saturday Review of Literature*, for the *Pisan Cantos* which Pound composed during that detention; and subsequently "in" and "out" and "in" once more. This intellectual cat-fight, including at least one public challenge to personal combat, has so totally befogged the issue under inky clouds of political righteousness, critical dogmas, and wounded *amour-propre* as to have moved the poet Karl Shapiro to declare in 1949 that "few poets anywhere"—let alone the perplexed layman!—"are in a position to say what they really think of Pound's work." Debates over literary (or other) personalities of the Twenties do not ordinarily bring into collision so wide a range of antipathies and loyalties—patriotic, cultural, political, ethnic, institutional, cultic, and personal—as the Pound controversy so notoriously has; but in lesser degree the reader must build his own defenses against the transient "ins" and "outs" of culture-criticism (including the present writer's) in assessing almost any career or creation of the Twenties.

One defense is to bear in mind the bewildering variety of what in fact was seen, done, heard, and read during the Twenties; its best-seller lists included both *Main Street* and Emily Post's *Etiquette*, both *The Story of Philosophy* and *Gentlemen Prefer Blondes*, both *Elmer Gantry* and *The Man Nobody Knows*, both *Magnificent Obsession* and *Believe It or Not*. They were banner years both for Ernest Hemingway and for Edgar Rice Burroughs, the creator of Tarzan. Another such check against the transitory critical absolutes is to study work which *was* the subject of high intellectual regard in the Twenties but has since been dropped from the canon; James Branch Cabell is a prime example. Booth Tarkington's reputation has suffered a similar eclipse even though the world of his novel *Alice Adams* "was, for incomparably more people than Spain or Paris or the Ritz could possibly be, the 1920's"; see Winfield Townley Scott, "Tarkington and the 1920's," *American Scholar*, XXVI (1957), 181–194. (There is of course the danger that such uncanonical writers may one day be restored to favor, but in the misleading form of "camp": Cabell, in his 1965 avatar as paperback science-fiction, may be an example.) One final check, as two novels cited by the writer in the text attest, is to pay some attention to the kind of art produced in the Twenties which by almost any standard in almost any period (except among our own "camp"-followers) could have been deemed "bad."

After such a plunge directly into the cross-currents of the Twenties—not before—is the time to turn to the many solid and valuable secondary accounts such as: Carl W. Condit, *American Building Art*, II: *The Twentieth Century* (New York, 1961); Blanche H. Gelfant, *The American City Novel* (Norman, Okla., 1954), a study the writer found particularly helpful on Dos Passos; Chadwick Hansen, "Social Influences on Jazz Style: Chicago 1920–30," *American Quarterly* XII (1960), 493ff.; Leland D. Peterson, "Ezra Pound: The Use and Abuse of History," *ibid.*, XVII (1965), 33ff.; or Philip M. Wagner, "Mencken Remembered," *American Scholar*, XXXII (1963), 256ff., to list only a few from a variety of fields. (Caution: lest any student receive the impression that books and ideas were all there were to the Twenties, let him read and reread Irving Bernstein's able and eloquent *The Lean Years: A History of the American Worker, 1920–1933* [Boston, 1960].)

In warning against taking the cultural life of the Twenties at second hand the present writer does not mean to imply that such accounts as, for example, Mark Schorer's monumental *Sinclair*

H

Lewis: An American Life (New York, 1961) can be dispensed with; quite the contrary. Nevertheless, even so careful and balanced a work as Schorer's has its own special pitfalls. As Andrew Sinclair wrote in the *Manchester Guardian Weekly* for November 15, 1962, reviewing a similarly careful and balanced and exhaustive study by Arthur and Barbara Gelb of Eugene O'Neill: "The effect of this gigantic biography is curious. . . . the sum of the facts do not add up to the whole O'Neill. In 'Long Day's Journey Into Night,' he reveals himself more nakedly than his biographers."

Indeed, for many of the leading figures of the Twenties—and this goes for politicians as well as for playwrights—the writer is tempted to violate one of the most axiomatic assumptions of his guild. "It goes without saying," as they say, that autobiography is inevitably self-serving, and never more artfully deceptive than when most "frank" and confessional; that the unpublished diary is more reliable than the most conscientious memoir, and the contemporary letter worth more credence still. But to shake one's faith in the relative credibility of diaries it is only necessary to think of Count Ciano's; and as for the utility of autobiography, who has more faithfully and accurately recorded the intentions of Herbert Hoover, for example, than Hoover's own *Memoirs*? The reader will have noticed that the writer has drawn heavily on autobiographies to invoke the spirit of the American Twenties; when they are as culturally lively as Matthew Josephson's engagingly titled *Life Among the SurRealists* (New York, 1962); as sexually frank as Max Eastman's *Love and Revolution: My Journey Through an Epoch* (New York, 1964); as judicious and common-sensical as *More Lives than One*, by Joseph Wood Krutch (New York, 1962); or as poignant as the memorable interview with Warren Harding that was recorded in *The Autobiography of William Allen White* (New York, 1946), their use for the interpretation of history requires no apology. They are cited especially in the first chapter of this work, out of a conviction that these reminiscent and articulate survivors by and large have been more insightful in their understanding of the period than are most of the younger people who write books about them.

Where the problem of interpretation becomes murky is the point at which conjuring up a mood passes over into judgment on controverted points of fact. Mr. Justice Frankfurter by consulting a clear and well-organized memory, and John Dos Passos by dusting off his own crumbling pamphlets and adding interpretive comment for the new age, can re-create a sense of what it felt like to work for the Sacco-Vanzetti Defense Committee; they cannot finally settle the question of which bullet could/might/must have been fired from whose revolver. Ballistics tests of "Sacco's" weapon in 1961—the quotation marks are a measure of the stubbornness of the controversy—only touched off a new round of argument; see Francis Russell, *Tragedy in Dedham: The Story of the Sacco-Vanzetti Case* (New York, 1962), and, in rebuttal, Michael A. Musmanno, "The Sacco-Vanzetti Case: A Critical Analysis of the book 'Tragedy in Dedham' . . .", 11 *Kansas Law Review* 481 (1963). Or, to take a less grim and racking example, it may well be true as Edgar Kauffmann and Ben Raeburn asserted, in *Frank Lloyd Wright: Writings and Buildings* (New York, 1960), that "Wright was able to recall the past with exceptional, detailed vitality" in his 1957 *Testament*—but do those buildings' roofs leak or don't they?

It is in forming this kind of judgment that the historian comes at last to play his indispensable role. He may not finally settle the controversy; indeed, he probably will not, but he can assist the reader to chart the controversy's shape and define its terms. For example, beginning with Samuel Lubell's discussion of it in *The Future of American Politics* (New York, 1952), one of the most central controversies about the Twenties, the presidential campaign of 1928, has received just such a clarifying treatment. Some of this analytical literature is cited in the notes to the present writer's "The Campaign of 1928 Re-Examined: A Study in Political Folklore," *Wisconsin Magazine of History*, XLVI (1963), 263ff. An aspect of the controversy not dwelt upon in that essay or in those cited sources was discussed by James H. Smylie in "The Roman Catholic Church, the State, and Al Smith," *Church History*, XXIX (1960), 321ff.; and an important more recent monograph is David Burner, "The Brown Derby Campaign," *New York History*, XLVI (1965), 356ff.

But no historian can have the last word on any debatable aspect of the Twenties by confining his attention to that brief decade alone. The John Kennedy episode has caused us to rethink the Al Smith episode; the affluence under Coolidge can instructively be compared with the affluence under Eisenhower; the stance of Secretary Kellogg is thrown into relief by the stance of Secretary Rusk. Indeed, for all the ritual absolution of themselves from the sin of "present-mindedness," all the discussants of the Twenties have brought the perspective of more recent events to bear. (It was the great merit of Henry May's essay to have pointed this out.) Most politically liberal historians, for example, consciously or unconsciously have judged the Twenties from their prior knowledge that the Crash was just around the corner; and when a conservative occasionally has contested this view (as in John Chamberlain, *The Enterprising Americans: A Business History of the United States,* New York, 1963, ch. 12), he like the liberals has ended by assessing the pre-Crash economy from the standpoint of a judgment on the coming events of the New Deal.

And if the New Deal has modified men's interpretation of the Twenties, so also has the Second World War; so too have the Cold War, the New Frontier, the Great Society. The Seventies and Eighties can be expected to contribute their own distinctive insights to an interpretation of the Twenties; and the next move, gentle reader, is up to you.

INDEX

Freudianism, 23, 58

Frost, Robert, 5, 16

Fundamentalism, 52, 54, 73, 78–86, 90

Furniss, Norman F., *quoted,* 78

Galbraith, John Kenneth, 6

Gallico, Paul, 21

Gandhi, Mohandas K., 47

Gangsters, Chicago, 73, 97

Garvey, Marcus, 92–93

Gasper, Louis, 79

Germany, 8, 11, 19–20, 46, 64, 82, 87, 89

Gernsback, Hugo, 7

Gibbons, Floyd, 44–45, 91

Gibbs, Philip, *quoted,* 1

Gibran, Kahlil, 13

Gilded Age, compared with Twenties, 1, 8–9, 10–11, 49, 67, 89

Ginger, Ray, 11, 68

Glad, *The Trumpet Soundeth,* 77

Glazer, *American Judaism, quoted,* 55

Glock and Stark, *Religion and Society in Tension, quoted,* 79

Goldwater, Barry, 70, 71, 76, 81

Gossett, *Race: The History of an Idea in America, quoted,* 90

Government in the Twenties
expansion of, 41–43, 45, 46, 47–48
reduction in scope of, 37–38, 40–41, 44, 56

Graham, Billy, 79

Grange, Red, 21, 32

Great Britain, 1, 11, 44, 47, 48, 50, 57, 68, 88

Green, Constance McLaughlin, *quoted,* 101

Hadley, Arthur Twining (in *Harper's,* 1925), *quoted,* 71

Hamilton, Alexander, 41

Handy, Robert T. (in *CH,* 1960), *quoted,* 52, 54

Hansen, Chadwick (in *AQ,* 1960), 103; *quoted,* 24

Harding, Warren G., 35, 38, 41, 56, 78, 92, 104

Harlem, 24, 62, 93

Harper's, 4, 17, 71

Hemingway, Ernest, 60–63, 65, 66, 103; *quoted,* 6, 60–61

Herbst, *The German Historical School in American Scholarship, quoted,* 89

Hibben, Paxton, 77

Hicks, Granville, 18

Hicks, John D., 2, 3; *quoted,* 36

Hoffman, *The Twenties,* 10, 11; *quoted,* 57

Hofstadter, Richard, *quoted,* 16, 31, 58–59, 68, 95

Holmes, John Haynes, *quoted,* 70

Holmes, Oliver Wendell, Jr., *quoted,* 93

Hoover, Herbert, 3, 43, 46, 47, 69, 75, 104; *quoted,* 6

Hoover, J. Edgar, 3

Hughes, Charles Evans, 76

Hughes, Langston, 62

Hunter, George William, *A Civic Biology* (1914), *quoted,* 83–84, 88–89

Huxley, Aldous, 7

Huxley, Julian, 57

Huxley, Thomas, 57

Immigration, 68, 87, 89, 90, 93–95, 97

India, 16, 47

Insull, Samuel, 32

Isolationism, 40, 43–47, 82

"Izzie and Moe" (Prohibition agents), 26

Jackson, Andrew, 4, 39, 76, 87, 97

Japan, 44–45, 48

World War II, 1, 44, 47, 48, 52, 60, 102, 106
Wright, Frank Lloyd, 86–88, 105
Wright, Richard, 18

YMCA survey, *Religion Among American Men, quoted,* 51

Youth, revolt of
in the Twenties, 1, 4, 5–6, 12–13, 52
in the Fifties and Sixties, 26, 67

Zieger, Robert H. (in *JAH,* 1965), *quoted,* 36